Turn Off The TV, Get Off Your Ass, and Do Something

Richard Lowe

The Writing King

Enemies of You Series

https://enemiesofyou.com

Turn Off The TV, Get Off Your Ass, and Do Something

Disclaimer

Not Medical or Professional Advice

This book reflects the author's observations, experience, and interpretation of available research. Where specific studies, statistics, or data are cited, the author has made reasonable efforts to represent them accurately. Readers who want to examine the underlying research will find key sources in the Further Reading section.

The suggestions in this book are not medical, psychological, financial, or legal advice. If you have concerns in any of those areas, consult a qualified professional. The changes described here, in how you use screens, manage your time, and direct your attention, are decisions you make for yourself, based on your own circumstances.

Results vary. What worked for the author and for the people he has worked with will not work identically for everyone. Some people have medical, professional, or personal reasons for their current digital habits that this book does not address. The goal is intentional use, not a universal prescription.

Table of Contents

See all books by Richard Lowe at

https://masterofworlds.com

Get free publishing insights and industry updates at

https://thewritingking.substack.com

For ghostwriting and book coaching services see

https://thewritingking.com

Enemies of You Series

———

Preface

This book started as a simple observation: most people complain about not having enough time while spending hours every day staring at screens. They say they're too busy to exercise, too tired to cook, too overwhelmed to read, and too stressed to spend time with friends. Then they watch Netflix for four hours.

Something doesn't add up.

I wrote the first version of this book in 2016, back when the biggest digital distraction was cable television and the occasional smartphone check. The world has changed dramatically since then. We now carry the entire internet in our pockets, work from our bedrooms, order everything through apps, and conduct relationships through screens.

What was a problem in 2016 has become a crisis in 2026.

This revised edition addresses the new landscape of digital dependency while keeping the argument that has remained true: the relationship between you and your technology is something you can change, and the changes that matter most do not require dramatic disruption of how you live.

What This Book Is

This is a practical guide for people who feel like their time is going somewhere they did not choose. People who scroll for an hour and feel nothing to show for it. People who have something they keep meaning to build and keep not building it. People who use technology all day and still feel like it is running them rather than the other way around.

The argument this book makes is specific. The problem is not screens. The problem is which side of the screen you are on. Every platform you use has a consuming side and a contributing side. On the consuming side, you are the audience: the product that platforms sell to advertisers, the attention that keeps the algorithm fed. On the contributing side, you are using the same tools to produce something: your own work, your own financial clarity, your own decisions made with better information. The device is identical. The relationship to it is not. This book is about crossing that line.

It is written for normal people living normal lives who use technology constantly and want to make sure it is working for them rather than the other way around. It is not an anti-technology book. It is an anti-passivity book. Those are different things, and the difference matters.

This is not a productivity hack book promising to optimize your life through better apps and systems. The solution is more thoughtful use of the technology you already have.

This is not a minimalism guide advocating for extreme lifestyle changes. You don't need to throw away all your devices and move to a cabin in the woods. Minor adjustments to digital habits can create significant improvements without requiring dramatic life changes.

The Further Reading section at the end of this book points to the most important research underlying its arguments, for anyone who wants to go deeper.

If you find a section that challenges your assumptions, that is the section worth sitting with longest.

A Warning About Perfection

One change made and held is worth more than ten changes planned and abandoned. The goal is not complete transformation on a schedule. It is a single adjustment that produces a different default, repeated until the default holds. Everything else follows from that, if it follows at all.

Who This Helps

This book is written for people who recognize themselves in the descriptions of passive consumption but are not sure where the useful pressure is. It is for people whose relationship with technology produces less than it costs, in time, in attention, in the slow erosion of things they meant to do. The argument it makes is specific enough to be useful and general enough to apply to almost any platform, any habit, any screen. The thousand hours in this book are an average, not a minimum. A parent with forty-five free minutes a night is working with a different number than a single person with four free hours. The redirect scales. Even five recovered hours a week, pointed at something real, compounds into a different year than the one the algorithm had planned for you.

How to Read This Book

You can read this book straight through or jump to chapters that address your concerns. Each chapter builds on previous concepts, but they're also designed to stand alone.

The first half of the book diagnoses problems with common digital habits. The second half provides practical alternatives and solutions. If you're already convinced that changes are needed, skip ahead to the solution chapters. If you are retired or no longer working, the chapters most directly relevant to your situation are 1 (Confessions of a Reformed Couch Potato), 4 (Your TV is Not Your Friend), 19 (The Couch Potato Diet), 21 (Conversations with Humans), 26 (Adventures in Going Outside), 29 (Make Something), 30 (Move Your Body), 31 (Build Real Friendships), 34 (Build Something Financially Real), and 36 (Find Your Community). The rest apply but may describe platforms or habits that are not part of your life. Start with the ones that are.

A Personal Note

I use digital tools from the moment I wake up until the moment I go to sleep. The difference between before and after 2014 is not how much I use technology. It is what I use it for. I make content; I do not primarily consume it. I open tools with a purpose; I close them when the purpose is done. That is the only change. It turns out to be sufficient.

The account in this book is personal and tested. The changes it describes are ones I made and have maintained. They are not theoretical. They are also not universal. What worked in my circumstances will not work identically in every circumstance, and the book is honest about that where it matters.

The Real Goal

The goal of this book is simpler than most books about digital habits: it is to make the line visible. The line between tools you are using and tools that are using you. Between hours you chose and hours the algorithm chose for you. Once you can see it clearly, the question of which side you are on becomes one you can answer. The rest follows from that.

Introduction

Why This Book Is Not What You Think It Is

Let me tell you what this book is not.

It is not a manifesto against technology. It is not asking you to throw your smartphone in a lake, cancel your subscriptions, and move to a cabin. It is not written by someone who thinks the internet was a mistake or that your life would be better if you went back to writing letters by candlelight.

I am not your enemy.

As of the time this book was written, I have over fifty books published, a ghostwriting business, a book coaching practice, a newsletter with tens of thousands of subscribers, and a full-time operation built on digital tools. I use AI for research, drafting, and editing. I publish through digital platforms. I communicate with clients through apps and messaging software. I have never once suggested that any of this was a mistake. The argument of this book is not that technology is the problem. The argument is that passivity is the problem, and that the tools most people are using primarily as an audience are the same tools others are using to build something.

Here is what this book is about.

In 2014, I unplugged my cable box and put it in a closet. People have been citing that fact ever since as evidence that I am anti-technology. They have it backwards. What I did that night was not turn off technology. What I did was stop being an audience member and start being a producer. The screens stayed on. The relationship to them changed entirely.

That is the only thing this book is about.

The line

There is a line that runs through every digital medium. On one side of that line, you are consuming. On the other, you are contributing. The screen is the same. The platform is the same. Your posture is not.

You can use YouTube to watch other people demonstrate skills you will never practice. Or you can use YouTube to teach the skills you have to an audience that cannot find them anywhere else. You can use social media to scroll through other people's edited lives and feel quietly inadequate. Or you can use it to build the audience for work you are making. You can use AI to have it think for you, write for you, and make decisions you were capable of making yourself. Or you can use it to amplify your own thinking: preparing for a difficult conversation, understanding a complex document, automating the admin that currently runs your evenings, or building the financial clarity that has been a vague source of anxiety instead of a known set of numbers.

The platform is neutral. Your relationship to it is not.

Most people are on the consuming side of every platform they use. Not because they are lazy or stupid. Because the algorithm has one job, and that job is to keep you there. Every feed, every recommendation engine, every autoplay feature is engineered to convert you into an audience member and keep you that way. The consuming side is the profitable side. The contributing side is where you stop being the product.

This book is a guide to crossing that line.

What that looks like

I did not become productive by giving things up. I became productive by changing what I was doing with the same hours. Before 2014, I spent roughly a thousand hours a year watching other people's creative work. After 2014, I spent those hours producing my own. The outputs are not the result of unusual discipline or talent. They are the result of redirecting a thousand hours a year from the consuming side to the contributing side, consistently, for a decade.

You do not need to write fifty books. But if you are reading this and you have something you have been meaning to make, the reason you have not made it is not that you lack the ability or the ideas. It is that a thousand hours a year are going somewhere else. This book is about where they are going, why, and what happens when you redirect them.

About AI

AI deserves a direct address here because it has changed this conversation significantly and it changes the question at the center of this book.

AI tools are the most powerful productivity amplifiers that have ever existed. A gig worker who uses AI to draft invoices, calculate quarterly taxes, and handle client communications in twenty minutes instead of three hours is getting their evenings back. A caregiver facing a complex medical situation who uses AI to research options and prepare the right questions walks into the doctor informed instead of overwhelmed. A small business owner who uses AI to handle the admin that used to eat every Sunday has recovered time they were not going to get any other way. A writer who uses AI to research, draft, and edit produces work that would have taken ten times longer. A teacher who uses AI to build courses reaches students they could not otherwise find.

That is one side of the line.

The other side is using AI as a replacement for your own thinking. Having it write things you never thought through. Using it to produce opinions you do not hold, in a voice that is not yours, about things you do not understand. Outsourcing judgment to a machine because judgment is uncomfortable. That version is not a creative tool. It is the most sophisticated passivity trap ever built: one that produces the feeling of having made something without the reality of it.

The test is simple: are you the author of what comes out, or is the machine? If you are providing the ideas, the judgment, the direction, and the expertise, and the tool is helping you produce and extend them, you are on the right side of the line. If you are prompting and accepting, you are on the consuming side of a platform that happens to produce text.

What you will find here

The first half of this book examines the major platforms and habits of modern digital life: television, the 24-hour news cycle, echo chambers, smartphones, social media, work messaging, streaming, gaming, sports betting, YouTube, TikTok, AI tools, podcasts, digital dating, and the financial mechanics of frictionless spending. Each chapter describes what the consuming side looks like, how the platform captures your attention and converts it into profit. But each chapter also shows you the contributing side: what it looks like when someone is using that same platform intentionally, to build something, to handle something, to learn something, or to produce something, rather than being processed by it as an audience member.

The second half is about active engagement, digital and physical. There are chapters on making things, moving your body, building real relationships, and finding community. There is a chapter about using digital tools to build something real. The argument of this book is not that screens are the problem. The argument is that passivity is the problem, and passivity is just as possible outdoors as it is on a couch.

The thirty-day plan at the end is not a detox. It is a redirect.

Who this is for

If you are happy with how you are spending your time, this book is not for you. If you feel like the hours are going somewhere you did not choose, and you have something you keep meaning to build, this book is for you.

You do not have to give anything up. You have to decide what you are building, and give the hours to that instead of to an algorithm that has no interest in what you build.

The line is there. You can step over it whenever you want.

Chapter 1: Confessions of a Reformed Couch Potato

Hello, my name is Richard, and I used to be a professional couch warmer.

I had shows. Important shows. Shows I would schedule my entire life around, as if they were medical appointments or court dates instead of fictional people doing fictional things for my fictional entertainment.

"Sorry, can't make dinner tonight. It's Thursday."

"What happens on Thursday?"

"My show is on."

"Can't you record it?"

Look of horror. "And watch it LATER? Like some kind of savage?"

I had achieved the pinnacle of modern living: completely up-to-date on the relationship drama of people who didn't exist, completely out of touch with the humans who did.

The Stepson Incident

My wake-up call came courtesy of my 19-year-old stepson, who had achieved the notable feat of being unemployed in Los Angeles, a city where you can get paid to stand on a street corner dressed as a hot dog.

I found him one afternoon horizontal on the couch, remote in hand, eyes glazed.

"Why aren't you in school?" I asked.

"Can we talk later? This is my favorite show."

"What about that job interview I set up?"

"They wanted me to work weeknight shifts."

"And?"

"That would interfere with Buffy the Vampire Slayer."

I stared at him. This young man had just turned down employment to watch a fictional blonde woman fight imaginary monsters. The thing is: I couldn't argue with his logic, because I had done the exact same thing approximately 847 times.

That moment landed differently than I expected. Not because my stepson was lazy. I had been just as lazy for years. But because standing there looking at him, I saw something I couldn't see when I was the one on the couch: we were both on the consuming side of something that had a contributing side. The same device. The same hours. Someone else was using them to make the show. We were using them to watch it.

That is the only distinction this book is about.

The Math

That night I did something dangerous: math.

Three hours of television a night is 21 hours a week. That's 1,092 hours a year, 27 full work weeks donated to the entertainment industry. I was a full-time professional viewer. Unpaid. Paying them.

So I unplugged the cable box and put it in a closet. No gradual reduction, no negotiation with myself. The screen went dark.

What came next was not rest. It was production. The hours did not disappear. They went somewhere else entirely. That redirection, not the abstinence, is the only thing this book is about.

The couch is still there. We're on good terms now. I sit on it to read or have conversations with people who exist. But it no longer has a television to answer to, and neither do I. One thing worth saying before the rest of the book begins: most passive consumption does not start with laziness. It starts with exhaustion. You come home depleted, and the screen is the easiest thing in the room. This book is not an argument against rest. It is an argument for noticing the difference between rest and disappearance.

Chapter 2: The Line

Consumer or Contributor: The Only Question That Matters

Here is something most books about digital distraction will not tell you: the problem is not the screen.

The screen is a tool. It is also a mirror, a stage, a distribution network, a classroom, a studio, and a marketplace. The same device that is making millions of people passive and isolated is also the tool that others are using to build businesses, teach skills to global audiences, write books, produce music, and create things that did not exist before they sat down with it. The device is identical. The relationship to it is not.

There is a line. On one side of that line, you are an audience member. On the other side, you are a contributor. Everything in this book is about which side of that line you are on when you pick up a device, and why that question matters more than how many hours you spend in front of a screen.

What the consuming side looks like

Most people are on the consuming side of every platform they use. This is not an insult, it is an accurate description of how these platforms are designed. The consuming side is the product that platforms sell to advertisers. Your eyes on content, your scroll time, your engagement rate, these are the raw material of a multi-trillion-dollar industry. Every feature of every major platform has been refined, through billions of dollars of behavioral research, to keep you in the audience seat and out of the production seat.

The consuming side of social media is scrolling through other people's lives, reacting to their posts, absorbing their opinions, and leaving with a vague sense of having been somewhere without having done anything. The consuming side of YouTube is clicking one recommended video, then another, then another, two hours later having watched a dozen creators demonstrate skills you will not practice. The consuming side of TikTok is letting an algorithm serve you an endless stream of fifteen-second emotional hits calibrated to your psychological profile until you look up and it is midnight. The consuming side of AI is typing a question and accepting the answer, outsourcing judgment to a machine because the machine is faster and judgment is uncomfortable.

None of this is difficult. It is designed not to be. The consuming side of any platform is always the path of least resistance, because the algorithm is a river and the current flows one direction.

What the contributing side looks like

The contributing side of the same platforms looks completely different.

The contributing side does not require an audience. It requires a purpose. The gig worker who uses AI to draft invoices and calculate their quarterly tax in twenty minutes instead of three hours is on the contributing side of technology. The person who opens a spreadsheet instead of a feed and knows where their money is going is on the contributing side. The caregiver who uses AI to research a medical diagnosis and walks into the doctor with the right questions is on the contributing side. So is the freelancer who automated their client follow-up, the student who built a study system that works, and the small business owner who finally got their admin under control. The contributing side also includes making things for others.

Social media used to build an audience for work you are doing. YouTube used to teach the skills you know better than most people. TikTok used to explain something clearly to the people who need to hear it. The contributing side of these platforms is real and accessible. But it is one expression of the same underlying principle: the tool is working for you, not the other way around.

You can use the same platforms that are passifying everyone else as the distribution infrastructure for work you are building. The infrastructure does not care what you do with it. Most people feed it. Some people use it.

AI: the most powerful tool ever built for people on the right side of the line

Artificial intelligence tools are currently at the center of a cultural panic running in two opposite directions at once. One camp says AI will replace all human creative work and render most people obsolete. The other camp says AI produces generic content and anyone using it is cheating. Both camps are missing the actual question, which is: what is your relationship to the output?

Here is the honest version.

AI amplifies what you bring to it. If you bring genuine expertise, hard-won experience, a specific voice, and real judgment about what is good, AI can help you produce work that reaches further and takes less time. The writer who knows their subject deeply and uses AI to research, draft, and edit is not being replaced. They are being amplified. The teacher who has spent twenty years developing a curriculum and uses AI to build courses, generate examples, and reach students they could not otherwise reach is not cheating. They are being extended. The consultant who uses AI to handle the analysis that used to take a junior associate three days is creating real advantage from real expertise.

If you bring nothing to it, if you use AI to generate opinions you have not formed, in a voice you have not developed, about subjects you have not studied, then what comes out is exactly what it looks like: confident-sounding text from a machine that has never thought about anything. Technically functional. Recognizably empty. And the audience can usually feel the difference, even when they cannot articulate why.

The test for whether you are on the contributing side of AI is simple: are you the author of what comes out? Not the typist, the author. Does it contain your thinking, refined by the tool? Or does it contain the tool's thinking, lightly steered by your prompt? The answer to that question is the line.

AI used well is a multiplier. You remain the thing being multiplied. The opportunity available to anyone on the contributing side of AI is greater than anything since the printing press made available to writers, greater than the recording studio made available to musicians. This is not hyperbole. It is arithmetic. If you are on the right side of the line, these tools are the most significant creative opportunity of your lifetime.

If you are using AI to replace your thinking rather than extend it, you are on the consuming side of the most sophisticated passivity trap ever built. One that produces the feeling of having made something without the reality of it.

Why the consuming side is the default

The consuming side is the default for a reason that has nothing to do with laziness. It is the default because it has been engineered to be substantially, deliberately, and continuously easier than the contributing side.

Starting something is hard. Opening a spreadsheet to look at your finances is harder than scrolling past the number. Setting up an invoicing system requires an afternoon that

Netflix does not. Learning the AI tool that would save you five hours a week takes an hour you keep not spending. Posting for the first time is awkward. The blank page is uncomfortable. The first video is embarrassing to watch back. The gap between where you are and where you want to be on the contributing side is real, and it does not close by itself.

Clicking play requires nothing.

I know this from the inside. For years I was a heavy consumer of television, which Chapter 1 covers at length. What I did not notice until I stopped was that the consuming side had been hiding the contributing side from me. The same hours, the same screen, the same device, and it had never occurred to me to flip the direction. That is the thing about a default: it does not feel like a choice.

The algorithm has no stake in you becoming a producer. Its stake is in keeping you in the seat you are in. This is why autoplay exists. This is why the feed is infinite. This is why every platform is designed to be easier to continue than to stop. The consuming side will always be there, always available, always easier. The contributing side requires a decision, made repeatedly, against the grain of the easier option being one swipe away.

How to read the rest of this book

The following chapters look at the major platforms and habits of modern digital life. Each one describes what the consuming side looks like, how it captures attention, how it is engineered for passivity, what it costs in time and cognitive capacity.

But each chapter also points to the other side. Not as a consolation prize, but as the actual point. The mechanisms described in the next chapter, the four ways digital platforms systematically capture and hold attention, are not reasons to reject the tools. They are the mechanisms that keep you on the consuming side of tools you could be using to produce something.

Every platform in this book has a consuming side and a contributing side. By the end of the book, you will know what both look like, and you will have a concrete plan for moving from one to the other.

The screen is the same. Your relationship to it is about to change.

Chapter 3: The Four Pillars of Digital Destruction

Four Mechanisms Every Platform Uses to Capture and Hold Your Attention

The chapters that follow examine specific platforms and habits in detail. Before getting there, it is worth naming the four mechanisms that almost all of them share. These are not accidents or side effects. They are documented, deliberate design features, refined through behavioral research to maximize the time a person spends on a platform. Knowing them does not make you immune to them. It does make the pattern visible, and once visible, it becomes harder to mistake the experience of being manipulated for the experience of choosing freely.

Pillar One: Time Theft

Time theft operates through a simple principle: digital platforms engineer the specific sensation of time passing without being noticed. You check the phone for a minute and an hour is gone.

The average American now spends over seven hours per day on screens. Over a year that is more than 2,500 hours, roughly 106 full days. Over a fifty-year adult life it compounds into more than fourteen years of waking time. The time does not feel stolen while it is happening. Every feature of the platform, autoplay, infinite scroll, the variable reward of the feed, is designed to make continuing easier than stopping. The disappearance is not accidental.

Pillar Two: Attention Span Destruction

The second mechanism is the systematic degradation of sustained attention. Human brains developed to focus deeply on single tasks for extended periods, the capacity that made complex problem-solving, learning, and creative work possible. Digital platforms erode this capacity by training the brain to expect constant novelty and to find sustained engagement with a single thing progressively uncomfortable.

The Stimulation Escalator

Every interaction with a digital platform is designed to deliver a small, immediate reward. The tap, the swipe, the notification check: each produces a minor dopamine response calibrated to encourage the next interaction. Brains exposed to this pattern repeatedly adapt to it. Tolerance for delayed reward decreases. Activities that produce results slowly, learning a skill, building a relationship, completing something difficult, begin to feel unreasonably effortful against the instant response the platform provides. This is the documented neurological mechanism, not a metaphor.

Pillar Three: Social Isolation

The research is consistent: increased digital connectivity correlates with increased feelings of loneliness and social isolation. The mechanism is the substitution of digital social contact for actual social contact.

The Parasocial Relationship Problem

Platforms create the feeling of connection through one-sided relationships with content creators and communities that recognize the user without knowing them. These relationships provide the emotional markers of belonging without the reciprocity, mutual vulnerability, or shared experience that real belonging requires. Over time, the low-friction version crowds out the high-friction one, not because anyone chose isolation, but because the digital alternative is always easier and always available.

The Performance Pressure

Social media compounds this by turning social interaction into performance. The post is crafted for an audience rather than directed at a specific person. The response is measured by engagement metrics rather than experienced as genuine exchange. The result is a generation with vast amounts of social-seeming activity and relatively little practice with the unedited, unscripted, real-time exchange that close relationships are built on.

Pillar Four: Comparison Culture

Platforms amplify the basic human tendency to compare ourselves to others, expanding the reference group from our immediate social circle to everyone online at once.

The Highlight Reel Effect

The fourth mechanism is the systematic amplification of social comparison. Platforms are designed to surface curated highlights: the vacation, the achievement, the flattering photograph. Nobody posts the ordinary Tuesday. The result is a continuous stream of other people's best moments against which a person measures their complete life, including all its Tuesdays. The comparison is structurally unfair and produces predictable dissatisfaction. Which the platforms profit from, because dissatisfied users scroll more, not less.

How the Pillars Work Together

These four mechanisms reinforce each other. Time loss makes attention damage harder to notice. Damaged attention makes social substitution more appealing. Social substitution feeds comparison, and comparison drives re-engagement. The loop is self-sustaining.

The chapters that follow describe what each of these mechanisms looks like inside specific platforms. The four pillars are how the consuming side keeps you there. Each chapter in the diagnosis section shows what they look like in practice, and what the other side of the same platform looks like when someone is using it with a purpose.

Chapter 4: Your TV is Not Your Friend

How the Design of Television Is Working Against You

Television is one of the older problems in this book, but it is not a solved one. The cable box in the closet has been replaced by the streaming subscription, and the streaming subscription has added a feature the cable box never had: it tracks precisely how long you watch, what you abandon, what you rewatch, and what keeps you from going to bed. It uses that data to serve you the next thing before you have decided whether you want it. The mechanism is more sophisticated than it was in 1990, but the core dynamic is the same: someone else is making the content, and you are providing the hours.

The Design of Television

Television shows are not designed to tell you a complete story and let you go on with your evening. They are designed to keep you watching. The cliffhanger, the cold open, the mid-season finale, the autoplay feature that starts the next episode before you have decided to watch it: these are not incidental to the medium. They are the product. The content is the delivery mechanism for the attention. Your attention is the thing being sold.

Netflix was explicit about this in a way that other entertainment companies were not. Their stated competitor was sleep. Not other networks, not other apps, sleep. The ambition was to be the thing people chose over the thing their bodies required. The business model depends on you staying longer than you intended.

What Television Actually Costs

By Nielsen's own measurements, the average American watches roughly five hours of television per day. Over a year, that is 1,825 hours, more than ten months of full-time work. Over a fifty-year adult life, it compounds into more than fourteen years of waking hours in front of a screen. This is not a metaphor designed to alarm. It is arithmetic.

The cost is not just time. It is cognitive state. Television watching is a low-arousal passive state, the brain is engaged but not directed, receiving but not producing. This is a categorically different use of your attention than the focused work of building something, the social engagement of a real conversation, or even the restorative idleness of a walk. The hours feel occupied while they are happening. They feel absent when you try to account for them.

I know this from the inside. When I was watching three hours a night, I was never bored. I was also never building anything. The two facts are related. Passive consumption is very good at occupying the time that creation would otherwise fill. It is engineered to make the competing alternative feel effortful by comparison.

The Attention Architecture

The structural features of television, narrative serialization, variable reward schedules, autoplay, the algorithm that selects your next show, are borrowed from and refined by the same behavioral psychology that powers every other platform in this book. The hook, the cliffhanger, and the next-episode preview are the television version of the notification, the like, and the infinite scroll. The goal is the same: make stopping feel harder than continuing.

Knowing this does not make you immune to it. But it changes the question from 'why can't I just watch one episode' to 'what is the system designed to make me do, and is that what I want.' Those are different questions. The second one has a better answer.

The hours are going somewhere every evening. They always have been. The question this chapter is asking is simply: do you know where they are going, and did you choose it? The person who made the show you just watched used hours exactly like that one to make it. The contributing side of television is the person who makes the show, not the person who schedules their week around watching it.

Chapter 5: Breaking News: The News is Breaking Your Brain

Why Watching Disaster Coverage 24/7 Won't Prepare You for Disasters

The news industry and the attention economy have the same business model: capture and hold your attention by making you feel like something important is always about to happen. The difference is that the news industry claims to be providing a public service while doing it, which gives the anxiety a moral justification. You are not scrolling for entertainment. You are staying informed.

This framing is worth examining. What most people mean by 'staying informed' is maintaining continuous awareness of events they cannot influence, delivered through a medium optimized for emotional arousal rather than comprehension. The result is not a well-informed population. Research on news consumption consistently shows that people who watch more television news are not better informed about factual matters than people who watch less. In some studies, they are worse informed, because the emotional intensity of the coverage displaces the substance of the information.

What the Business Model Requires

Broadcast news is paid for by advertising. Advertising revenue is proportional to viewership. Viewership is proportional to engagement. Engagement is highest when the viewer is anxious, outraged, or afraid. The editorial choices that follow from this structure are not the result of individual bad intentions. They are the rational output of an incentive system.

The car chase coverage, the weather catastrophizing, the expert panel speculating about events that happened four hours ago with no new information: these are not failures of journalism. They are the product working as designed. A channel that covered only events that materially affected your daily life, at the pace at which those events developed, with the degree of uncertainty that exists, would lose viewers to the channel that made everything feel urgent and personal.

The result is a medium that is very good at making you feel activated and very poor at helping you understand anything. The activation is the product. The understanding was never the goal.

The Anxiety Accumulation

People who consume daily news report higher levels of anxiety about events than people who do not, without corresponding higher levels of accurate knowledge about those events. This is not surprising given what the medium is optimized to produce. What is surprising is how rarely people connect their daily news consumption to their daily mood.

I stopped consuming mainstream news regularly about ten years ago. I did not stop caring about what happens in the world. I became more deliberate about how I found out. Trade publications for my industry. Long-form journalism with named sources and editorial standards. Local government meetings, which tell you more about what is happening in your community in two hours than a year of local news broadcasts. Conversations with people who have direct knowledge of the things I need to understand.

The things that mattered still reached me. Genuinely important events are impossible to avoid. They enter the ambient conversation, they come up in interactions, they cannot be missed. What stopped reaching me was the manufactured urgency around events that did not require my emotional investment. My mood improved measurably. My actual knowledge of things that affected my life did not decrease.

The anxiety that news consumption produces is not proportional to events. It is proportional to the medium. The same events covered in a ten-minute weekly summary produce a fraction of the psychological load of the same events covered continuously across a twelve-hour day. The medium is calibrated for arousal, not comprehension. Opting out of the medium is not opting out of the world. It is opting out of the arousal.

The Withdrawal

People who stop consuming daily news consistently report the same sequence: first, low-grade anxiety about being uninformed. Then, within a few weeks, the realization that genuinely important things still reach them. Then, the discovery that the mood improvement is real and measurable. The anxiety they attributed to the state of the world was partly the anxiety of consuming a medium engineered to make them anxious. Removing the medium removes a significant portion of the load.

From consuming news to making it

The most reliable antidote to bad news consumption is firsthand participation in how things work. The person who attends a city council meeting knows more about local government in two hours than a year of local news broadcasts provides, because the meetings are where the decisions get made, and the news covers the drama rather than the substance. Attending, participating, and occasionally speaking is a form of contribution that the passive news consumer never makes.

There is also a contributing side to journalism itself. Local reporting is genuinely underfunded and the gap between what is happening in most communities and what is being covered is large and growing. A person with a newsletter, a podcast, or even a consistent social media presence focused on their local area can fill parts of that gap. The bar for doing it better than the average local news broadcast is lower than it appears.

The shift from consuming national news to contributing to local information, attending meetings, publishing observations, documenting things that would otherwise go undocumented, is one of the more direct redirects available. The news that affects your daily life is local. The local information ecosystem is the one where a single person's contribution makes a measurable difference.

The Choice

The daily dose of news does not make you better prepared for the things that affect your life. It makes you more anxious about the things that do not. The people who stepped back from daily consumption did not become ignorant of events that mattered. They became calmer about events that did not concern them. Which is most of what the news covers.

The news will still be there if you want it. Genuinely important events will reach you regardless. But the daily psychological toll of treating every story as a personal emergency, that you can opt out of.

The contributing side of news is the person who writes something about what they think, not the person who absorbs other people's reactions to events at volume.

Chapter 6: Welcome to Your Personal Echo Chamber

Where Everyone Agrees with You and Reality is Optional

Every platform you spend time on has been designed to show you what keeps you there longest. Not what is most true, most useful, or most important to you. What is most likely to produce another click, another scroll, another minute of engagement. Over time, this design does something specific to how you understand the world: it builds a version of reality optimized for your continued presence on the platform, not for your actual comprehension of events.

The result is not stupidity. It is a highly personalized information environment that feels like staying informed while functioning more like a mirror. You are not seeing the world. You are seeing the world as the algorithm predicts you want to see it. Those are not the same thing, and the gap between them widens every time you engage.

The Algorithm Knows You Better Than You Know You

The mechanism is simple. Every click, share, and extended view tells the algorithm something about what keeps you engaged. The algorithm responds by showing you more of that. Political anger produces more political anger. Generational grievance produces more generational grievance. Nutrition certainty produces more nutrition certainty. The loop has no correction built into it because correction, encountering a view that challenges yours, sitting with ambiguity, updating your position, reduces engagement. The algorithm is not trying to inform you. It is trying to retain you. Those are opposite goals.

I noticed this most clearly in myself around 2020, when I realized that every time I looked up a news event, the subsequent days would fill with content about that event from a very particular angle. Not because that angle was correct. Because it was the angle I had clicked on first. The feed had learned my bias and was deepening it in real time.

The Confirmation Loop

The feed does not show you a representative sample of views on any topic. It shows you the content that your prior engagement predicts you will engage with again. Since most people engage more with content that confirms their positions than with content that challenges them, the feed learns to confirm. The result is an information environment that feels diverse, many different people, many different stories, but is ideologically monotone.

You are not seeing the world. You are seeing a mirror of your own prior reactions, served back to you at scale.

What Outrage Is For

Anger is one of the most reliable engagement signals available to the algorithm. People who are angry share more, comment more, and spend more time on platform than people who are merely informed or entertained. This is not a side effect of social media design; it is a load-bearing feature. Platforms that optimized for positive emotion did not achieve the same retention. The ones that succeeded at scale discovered that low-level sustained outrage is a more dependable product than satisfaction. The practical consequence is a feed calibrated to find whatever makes you angry and serve you more of it. This is not a conspiracy. It is an optimization function running on engagement data. The algorithm is not trying to make you angry. It is trying to retain you, and anger retains you. The distinction matters because it means the fix is not about platform moderation or content policy. It is about whether you want to be retained by something whose incentive is your outrage.

I deleted the news app from my phone in 2019. Not because the news was bad, the news was the news, but because I noticed I was checking it the way I used to check the television: reflexively, repeatedly, and with diminishing returns on actual information. I was not getting more informed. I was getting more activated. Those are not the same thing.

The Credibility Shortcut

The echo chamber does not just confirm your positions. It supplies apparent authorities to confirm them for you. The algorithm surfaces people with credentials, titles, and confident delivery who hold positions compatible with your existing views. The credential may be real; it may also be entirely unrelated to the subject at hand. A physician commenting on monetary policy, an economist commenting on vaccine efficacy, a lawyer commenting on climate modeling, the title travels across domains in a way that actual expertise does not. The algorithm does not distinguish. It surfaces whoever produces the kind of engagement that keeps you watching. The practical effect is that people come away from their feeds feeling that their positions are expert-backed when they are personality-backed. Expert-backed positions are revisable when evidence changes. Personality-backed positions are defended against contradicting evidence, because the attachment is social rather than epistemic. The feed did not give you a better-informed view. It gave you a tribe with credentials attached.

The Complexity Cost

Most policy questions involve genuine trade-offs: things that are good in some ways and bad in others, depending on which values you weight and which outcomes you care about. The algorithm cannot serve this complexity at scale because ambivalent, careful content does not produce reliable engagement. What produces engagement is moral clarity: the other side is not just wrong, they are bad. You are not just right, you are good.

People emerge from years of algorithm-curated news with positions that are strong and brittle at the same time: confidently held and poorly stress-tested. They have been shown, repeatedly, that their instincts are correct and the other side's motives are suspect. They have not been shown the version of the opposing argument that a thoughtful person believes. That version does not perform well enough to surface.

Confirmation Hunting

Most people who believe they have researched a topic have done something different: they have searched for confirmation of what they already suspected, found it, and stopped looking. This is not stupidity. It is the path of least cognitive resistance, and the algorithm is engineered to make that path feel like thoroughness. You searched, you found sources, you read them. That feels like research. But if every source agreed with you before you arrived, you have not tested your position. You have photographed it from a flattering angle.

Real research is uncomfortable. It requires finding the strongest version of the argument you disagree with and engaging with it, not the weakest version your feed serves up to make the other side look foolish. Most people have not encountered the strongest version of positions they oppose, because the algorithm has no incentive to show it to them.

The Conversation Killer

The practical consequence of years of algorithm-curated information is a specific kind of confidence: positions held with certainty but without the load-bearing structure that makes certainty defensible. People know what they believe. They have seen enormous amounts of content confirming it. They have not encountered the strongest version of the argument against it, because that version does not perform well enough to surface. When they meet someone who disagrees, the disagreement registers as unreasonableness rather than as a different set of information or values. The conversation becomes a correction rather than an exchange. Nobody's position moves.

The Confidence Problem

The echo chamber does something specific to your relationship with certainty. Genuine experts in almost any field become more careful about their claims as they learn more, because they develop a clearer sense of what the evidence supports and what it does not. The algorithm-fed reader develops the opposite: conviction without the load-bearing structure that makes conviction defensible. I have had conversations with people who were absolutely certain about epidemiology, monetary policy, and climate modeling, subjects that take careers to understand, because they had consumed a great deal of content that agreed with a particular position. The content was not necessarily wrong. But their certainty was borrowed rather than earned, and borrowed certainty is brittle. It holds up fine until someone asks a question the feed never thought to answer.

The echo chamber does not fail you because you are seeing too little content. It fails you because the content has already been filtered for compatibility with your existing positions. More content from more sources, if still routed through the same algorithm, produces more of the same filtering at higher volume.

The actual antidote is accountability to an audience that does not already agree with you. Which is why the contributing side of the information problem is not consuming differently, but producing something that has to survive contact with genuine disagreement.

Publishing your way out of the echo chamber

The most effective way to break out of an echo chamber is to publish your actual views under your own name to a general audience. The algorithm shows you what it predicts you want to see. Publishing to a real audience, one that includes people who disagree, forces the opposite: you encounter genuine pushback, you learn where your reasoning is weak, you develop the ability to defend positions rather than just hold them. The accountability of public writing is a feature, not a bug.

Content that deliberately engages with multiple perspectives, not to seem balanced, but because the subject genuinely requires it, is also among the most valuable things a creator can do for an audience that is tired of being sorted into camps. The creator who can explain why reasonable people disagree about something, fairly, is providing something the algorithm actively suppresses. That gap is real and the audience for it is larger than the engagement metrics suggest.

The Choice

The contributing side of the echo chamber problem is not consuming more diverse content. It is producing content that you have to own, that you have to defend, and that reaches people who did not already agree with you before they arrived.

The information environment you inhabit is not neutral. It has been calibrated, continuously and automatically, to confirm what you already believe. Knowing this is the beginning of choosing differently. The contributing side of the echo chamber is the person who publishes something under their own name that people who disagree can find and respond to, not the person consuming a feed that was designed to never show them anything that would require them to change their mind.

Chapter 7: Smartphone Zombies and Other Modern Wildlife

A Field Guide to Humans Who've Forgotten How to Walk Without Staring at Screens

The smartphone changed the relationship between people and their attention in a way that is still working itself out. The device is not simply a communication tool that also happens to have entertainment on it. It is an attention-capture device that also happens to make calls. The distinction matters because it determines how you think about having it in your pocket at all times.

The data on how people use phones has been consistent for years. The average person checks their phone around 96 times per day, once every ten minutes during waking hours. Most of those checks are not purposeful. They are habitual: the hand reaches for the device before the mind has decided to. That reflex is not a character flaw. It is the product of a system deliberately designed to produce it, using the same variable-reward psychology that makes slot machines hard to walk away from.

I have caught myself checking my phone within thirty seconds of putting it down. Not because something important was incoming, nothing was, but because the habit had its own momentum. The check and the reflex had become the same thing. That is the design working as intended.

The Notification Pavlov

The mechanism that makes the phone hard to put down is the same mechanism that makes slot machines hard to walk away from: intermittent variable reinforcement. Most checks of the phone produce nothing significant. Occasionally one produces something genuinely interesting. The unpredictability is the feature, not a flaw. A phone that delivered only relevant information would be checked far less often. A phone that sometimes delivers something rewarding, on a schedule you cannot predict, will be checked compulsively, because that is what brains do with variable reward schedules. The design team knew this. The behavior is the intended outcome.

The Texting Shift

The migration from voice calls to text messages is not simply a change in communication format. It is a change in the kind of communication that happens. A phone call is a real-time exchange that requires presence, responsiveness, and the management of silence. A text message is asynchronous, editable, and deniable. It can be composed over twenty minutes and delivered in seconds, presenting the impression of spontaneity while allowing the complete elimination of the risk of actual spontaneity.

The result is communication that is more frequent and less substantive. Most people now send dozens of messages a day that would not have been sent at all in a previous era, because the friction of a phone call would have filtered them out. This volume of low-content exchange creates a simulation of constant connection that substitutes for the occasional high-content exchange that connection requires.

The Performance Loop

The shift from experiencing something to documenting something for an audience is one of the subtler costs of the smartphone era. It is not that documentation is bad. It is that the documentation reflex, once established, operates on everything, including experiences where its presence is a direct cost to the quality of the experience itself. A concert attended through a phone screen is a concert at which you were present and absent at once. The video exists. The experience was replaced by the production of the video.

Social media created an incentive structure that rewards documentation over experience, because documentation is shareable and experience is not. The platform gets engagement from the post. The person gets the feeling of having shared something. The actual event is the least important thing in the transaction.

The Spatial Dependency

Navigation is a small example of a larger pattern. The smartphone has not just added convenience to tasks humans already performed, it has replaced the underlying capability entirely for many people. The ability to find your way somewhere, hold a phone number in memory, do arithmetic without a calculator, sit with a question before looking it up, all of these have been outsourced so completely that the skill atrophies within a few years of disuse. This is not catastrophic. But it means the device has moved from optional to structural in a way that most people did not consciously choose. You did not decide to become unable to handle without GPS. It happened gradually, one turn-by-turn at a time, while you were thinking about something else.

The Attention Span Collapse

The smartphone has accelerated something that used to take years, the erosion of your ability to sit with a thought for longer than forty-five seconds. Every ping, buzz, and notification is a tiny interruption that resets your concentration clock. Do this ninety-six times a day, every day, for years, and your brain rewires itself. Tasks that require sustained focus, reading a chapter, following a complex argument, doing deep work, start to feel physically uncomfortable, in a way that feels structural rather than momentary. You don't know why you can't concentrate. You just know you keep picking up your phone.

The Bedroom Problem

The phone on the nightstand is doing two things at once: it is a source of stimulation immediately before sleep, and it is the first input of the morning before the brain has had any unoccupied time. Both of these are structurally corrosive to the kind of rest Chapter 27 describes, the kind that restores rather than merely passes the hours. Blue light and cognitive activation before sleep are well-documented sleep disruptors. Less discussed is the subtler effect: the person who checks their phone before bed and first thing in the morning never fully leaves the feed. The day begins with other people's agendas and ends with them. The unoccupied space where the mind processes what happened and prepares for what comes next, that space has been colonized. The phone does not have to be a problem you can see for it to be a problem.

The Phantom Vibration Syndrome

One of the more telling signs that the relationship with the device has become compulsive is the experience of phantom vibration: the sensation that the phone is buzzing when it is not. The nervous system has been trained to anticipate the signal so reliably that it generates false positives. This is not a metaphor for dependency. It is physiological evidence of it, the body adapting to an environmental stimulus the same way it adapts to any other repeated pattern.

The Watch That Watches You

The smartphone is not the only screen on your body anymore. Tens of millions of people now wear a device on their wrist that monitors their heart rate, sleep stages, blood oxygen, step count, stand hours, exercise minutes, heart rate variability, and estimated calories burned, continuously, throughout the day and night. The Apple Watch, Oura Ring, WHOOP band, and Fitbit collectively represent a category that barely existed a decade ago and now generates billions of dollars annually. The pitch is simple: knowledge is health. Track everything, improve everything, live better.

The reality for a significant number of users is more complicated. Therapists working with anxiety disorders report a specific new presentation: patients who cannot fall asleep because they are worried about their sleep score. People who wake in the night and immediately check their wearable to see how the sleep is going, thereby destroying the sleep they were trying to optimize. People who cancel rest days from exercise because their recovery score suggests they should be ready to train, overriding what their body is telling them. People who check their resting heart rate multiple times per day, interpreting normal variation as evidence of a health problem requiring attention.

There is a clinical pattern of health anxiety amplified by constant body monitoring, sometimes called health anxiety or cyberchondria when driven by medical information, but the wearable-specific version has no single diagnostic label yet. What it looks like in practice is this: the device was purchased to improve health, but it has instead created a new source of chronic low-level anxiety about the body. The person wearing it knows more about their biometrics than any previous generation of humans has known about their bodies, and they are often less comfortable in their body than they were before they started tracking it. This is the smartphone dependency pattern expressed through health.

The same mechanism, constant data availability creating compulsive checking behavior, which generates anxiety rather than information, operates through a wristband instead of a news feed. The variable reward is not a like or a notification; it is a good sleep score or a high HRV reading. The punishing signal is not an argument in the comments; it is a poor recovery percentage that sends someone into a spiral of interpretation and preemptive intervention.

Wearables are not inherently harmful. For people managing specific health conditions, monitoring cardiac arrhythmias, or training for endurance events, the data is genuinely useful. The problem is when continuous biometric surveillance migrates from a tool that informs specific decisions into a compulsive behavior that substitutes quantitative data for the body's own signals.

You knew how you felt before you checked the app. If you are checking the app because you no longer trust how you feel, the device has not made you healthier. It has made you dependent.

The smartphone as production studio

The device described throughout this chapter is also the most powerful creative production tool ever made available to people at no cost. Every person reading this has a camera, a microphone, a word processor, a publishing platform, a distribution network, and an AI assistant in their pocket. The smartphone zombie described above and the creator who built a real business from their phone are using identical hardware. The difference is entirely in the relationship to the device.

Documentary photographers now shoot on phones. Podcasters record on phones. Writers draft on phones. Course creators film on phones. The technical barrier between having something worth saying and reaching an audience for it has effectively disappeared. What remains is the decision about which side of the screen to be on, the side that consumes what others have made, or the side that makes things for others to find.

The cure for smartphone addiction is not a dumber phone. It is a purposeful one, where you open it to produce something specific, finish that thing, and close it again. The difference between the device running your life and the device serving your work is not a hardware problem. It is a relationship problem, and relationships can be changed.

The Cure

The phone in your pocket is the most capable tool your generation has ever had access to. The people who built significant things from it did not do so by using it less. They did so by using it with a specific direction in mind before they opened it. Open it for a reason. Do that thing. Close it. The device does not change. The relationship to it does. That is the only fix that has ever worked, and it works completely.

Chapter 8: Social Media: The Greatest Antisocial Invention Ever

How We Got 500 "Friends" and Zero Real Conversations

Social media platforms describe themselves as connection tools. The description is accurate in a narrow sense: they do connect people, in the same way that a waiting room connects people. Everyone is in the same space. Nobody is talking. The architecture of these platforms, the feed, the metric, the performance for an audience rather than exchange with a person, is optimized for engagement, not connection. Those are not the same thing, and the data showing rising loneliness alongside rising social media use is the clearest evidence of the difference.

The Friendship Inflation

Social media platforms use the word 'friend' to describe relationships that span an enormous range of actual closeness, from people you speak to weekly to people you met once a decade ago. This conflation benefits the platform: a network with 500 friends feels more valuable than one with 12 acquaintances and 2 actual friends, even if the genuine relationships are identical. The inflation is good for metrics. It is not an accurate picture of your social life.

The Performance Theatre

Every post is a edited selection, the best photograph from forty attempts, the achievement rather than the ordinary day, the gathering where everyone is smiling rather than the argument that happened in the car on the way there. This is not dishonesty so much as the natural incentive of a system that rewards engagement: posts that make life look enviable perform better than posts that make life look accurate. The audience scrolling through the feed is comparing their complete, unedited experience against everyone else's edited presentation. The comparison is structurally rigged.

The Validation Addiction

The like, the share, the comment are operant conditioning mechanisms calibrated for maximum engagement. The platform does not care whether you feel better or worse after checking your metrics. It cares whether checking brings you back. Which it reliably does. A system that rewards you sometimes and produces nothing other times is more addictive than one that rewards consistently. This is slot machine psychology applied to social approval, and the people who designed these systems understood exactly what they were building.

The Echo Chamber Amplifier

The echo chamber amplification built into social media makes disagreement feel like malfunction. The person whose feed has consistently confirmed their positions encounters someone who disagrees and experiences it as surprising, even offensive, rather than as the expected encounter with a person with different information or different values. Nobody changes their mind. Nobody's relationship deepens. The platforms have not produced a more polarized society by intention, but they have as a consequence of optimizing for the engagement that outrage and tribal confirmation reliably generate.

The Outrage Manufacturing Plant

Outrage is the most reliable engagement signal available to the algorithm. The platform does not decide to make you angry. It optimizes for the behavior that makes you stay, and staying is what anger produces. The person who is calm and informed scrolls past. The person who is angry clicks, shares, and comments. Every share extends the session for the sharer and adds impressions for the platform.

The outrage is not a side effect. It is the product, in the same sense that anxiety is the product of the news industry.

The Productivity Vampire

The time cost is the most legible part of the cost. Two hours per day is 730 hours per year, more than eighteen standard work weeks. The platforms celebrate this. 'Daily active users' and 'time on platform' are their primary success metrics because you are the product and your time is the raw material. That is not a metaphor. It is the precise economic relationship.

The Comparison Trap

The comparison mechanism is structural, not incidental. The feed surfaces other people's best moments continuously, the vacation, the achievement, the gathering where everyone is smiling. Nobody posts the ordinary Tuesday. A person scrolling through the feed is comparing their complete, unedited experience against hundreds of edited presentations at once. The comparison is always going to produce dissatisfaction, which is precisely why the platform profits from it: dissatisfied users scroll more, not less.

The Conversation Killer

The specific loss is reciprocal exchange: the kind of conversation where both people leave knowing something they did not know before, where a position sometimes changes because the other person made a better argument, where the relationship deepens through genuine contact rather than parallel performance. Social media is structurally incompatible with this. It rewards volume over depth, certainty over curiosity, and the performance of a position over its actual examination.

The Career You're Posting Away

Social media has produced a category of self-inflicted professional disaster that did not exist twenty years ago: the person who posts themselves out of a job, a career, or a future. This is not a rare occurrence. Employment attorneys have made it a specialty. HR departments have written policies for it. Journalists cover new examples every week. The pattern is consistent enough that it has become a predictable occupational hazard, and yet people keep walking into it with their phones raised.

The firing variant is the most immediate. The employee who records a confrontation with their manager and posts it to TikTok while still in the building. The nurse who films patients without consent for content. The retail worker who live-streams their shift from the stockroom. The server who posts video of difficult customers. In each case, the person believes they are making relatable content, or documenting an injustice, or simply sharing something funny. What they are doing is creating a permanent public record that violates confidentiality agreements, privacy laws, or basic professional standards, often all three at once, and handing it to anyone who wants to use it against them. The termination meeting usually happens within 24 hours. Sometimes within the hour.

The longer-term version is quieter and more widespread. Employers now routinely search job applicants on social media before interviews. Research consistently finds that the majority of employers screen job applicants' social media profiles during the hiring process. What they find is often disqualifying not because the applicant did anything illegal, but because the accumulated public record of their opinions, jokes, photographs, and associations from the last five to ten years paints a picture that no reasonable employer wants attached to their organization. The post you made at 23 that seemed edgy and funny is still there at 31

when you are applying for something that matters. The photograph from the party you thought was private was shared by someone who did not share your privacy settings. The argument you had publicly on Twitter in 2019 about something you no longer even remember is indexed and searchable. The internet does not forget, and it does not accept the defense that you were younger then.

There is a specific sub-category that deserves its own sentence: the person who films their own firing. It happens. People have their phones out during termination meetings, disciplinary proceedings, and HR conversations, recording what they believe is evidence of unfair treatment. Sometimes it is. More often, the recording itself violates the terms of their employment agreement and transforms a potentially contestable dismissal into an open-and-shut one. The camera that was supposed to protect them made their situation worse. The impulse to document, to capture, share, and validate, overrode the judgment that some moments are not content.

The culture that trained people to perform constantly for an audience of followers has not provided them with a reliable instinct for when the performance should stop. The result is a pattern that cuts across generations: people who have documented their way into genuinely preventable professional consequences, one post at a time, because the habit of sharing everything has outlasted any consideration of what everything means.

The Privacy Paradox

The data collection model of social media is worth naming plainly: you are not the customer of these platforms. You are the product. The information you generate through your posts, your clicks, your location, and your behavioral patterns is what the platform sells to advertisers. The social experience is the mechanism by which that data is collected. This arrangement is disclosed in the terms of service that almost nobody reads, and it is the foundational economic fact of how every major social platform operates.

The Real Social Alternative

The platforms have been effective at providing a social experience that requires nothing from you. You can be connected to hundreds of people without being present with any of them. The alternative, actual contact with actual people, including the awkwardness and the effort and the possibility of genuine exchange, is harder and produces more. The person who stops scrolling and calls someone does not lose the connection the platform was providing. They replace it with something the platform cannot replicate.

I had a Facebook account for about three years before I deleted it. During that time I accumulated 340 "friends," none of whom called when I stopped posting. Which tells you exactly what the word means in that context. What I noticed after deleting it was not that I missed the platform, I missed nothing about it, but that I started calling people instead of passively monitoring them. Those calls led to actual plans. The plans led to actual time together. The time together reminded me what I had been substituting scrolling for.

The Choice

The platforms provide a low-friction version of the thing humans need: genuine contact with other people over time. The low-friction version is always available, never awkward, and produces none of the compounding benefit that the real thing does. The people who stopped scrolling and started calling, visiting, and showing up are not discovering something new. They are rediscovering what was always true about how connection works.

The active side of social media

The same platforms described in this chapter have also produced the largest democratization of distribution in history. Before social media, reaching an audience required a publisher, a record label, a television network, or a newspaper. Now a person with genuine expertise, a real story, or a useful skill can build a following of thousands or millions without institutional permission. This is not nothing. It is, in fact, a real thing. The difference between the social media user who ends the evening feeling worse and the one who ends it having moved something forward is the direction of the transaction. One is taking in, scrolling, reacting, absorbing, comparing. The other is putting out, sharing something made, teaching something learned, building something that compounds. The platform is identical. The posture is opposite.

If you spend time on social media, the productive question is not how to use it less. It is what you are contributing. If the answer is nothing, the chapter above is your diagnosis. If you have something to say, something to teach, or something to build, social media is a distribution network waiting to be used, not just a feed waiting to consume you.

Social media is a tool that became a habitat for most of the people using it. The person who built an audience on it, published work through it, or used it to reach people who needed what they had to say. They used the same platform, the same hours, the same phone. The contributing side of social media is the person other people are following, not the person doing the following. One qualification: following with purpose, studying a specific skill, tracking a field you work in, learning from someone who knows more than you, is a different activity from ambient scrolling through a feed. The test is whether you chose the person and the topic before you opened the app, or whether the algorithm chose for you after you did.

Chapter 9: Pajama Professionals and the Death of Real Meetings

How Remote Work Turned Your Home Into a Screen You Can't Turn Off

Before 2020, most people had at least one reliable daily break from screens: the commute. Not the part where you sat in traffic watching a podcast, but the physical act of leaving one place and going to another. You walked to a car, a bus stop, a train platform. You moved through the world. You arrived somewhere that was not your bedroom. And when the workday ended, you did it in reverse, and the act of crossing the threshold into your home signaled, physically and psychologically, that work was over.

Remote work eliminated that boundary. Not gradually, but overnight, for tens of millions of people at once. The bedroom became the office. The kitchen table became the conference room. And the home, which had been the one place in daily life where you were allowed to be something other than productive, became colonized by screens that never turned off. Your laptop was now three feet from where you slept. Your phone was always "for work." The line between screen time you chose and screen time you owed dissolved entirely.

This is the chapter about remote work, but it is not really about productivity or pajamas. It is about what happens when every room of your home becomes a screen environment, when there is no physical place you can go in your daily life that is not an invitation to be online, and when the last reliable reason to exist in the physical world, going to a job, disappears from your daily schedule.

The Great Pajama Migration

Remote work did not eliminate the office environment. It relocated it into every room of the home. The workspace previously contained behind a commute and a building entrance now occupies the kitchen table, the bedroom, and the couch at once. The physical boundary that used to signal the transition between working and not-working disappeared, and with it, one of the more reliable mechanisms for leaving work behind.

The Zoom Zoo

Video conferencing introduced a new variable into professional meetings: the performance of attention. The camera shows the face but not the second screen. It shows the expression but not the other tab that is open. The meeting becomes a setting in which physical presence is simulated while mental presence is optional, and everyone in the meeting knows this about everyone else without saying so. The social norm of pretending full attention is present when it is not is a specific cost of remote collaboration that rarely appears in the productivity analyses.

The Multitasking Myth

The home environment introduces a specific category of competition for attention that the designed office environment eliminates: domestic life. The task waiting in the kitchen. The package arrival. The ambient domestic sound. An office is engineered, deliberately, at significant cost, to suppress exactly this category of distraction. Working from home removes that engineering and replaces it with nothing except individual discipline, which is a much less reliable substitute.

The Isolation Station

The office provides incidental social contact that remote work eliminates: the hallway conversation, the lunch, the informal exchange that is not a meeting and does not appear on the calendar. This contact is not merely pleasant. It is load-bearing in professional relationships. Trust and collaboration develop through accumulated small interactions over time, not through scheduled video calls. The research on remote teams consistently finds that the deficit is real and compounds as the period of remote work extends.

The Productivity Paradox

The productivity question is genuinely mixed. Jobs requiring deep individual focus and minimal coordination often work well remotely. Jobs requiring frequent collaboration, spontaneous problem-solving, or the transfer of tacit knowledge between people tend not to. The blanket claims in either direction do not survive contact with the actual research, which shows significant variation by role, individual, and organizational context.

I work from home and have for most of my career. The discipline that makes it work is not discipline about output. It is discipline about structure: a defined workspace, defined hours, and a hard stop that signals the workday is over.

The Communication Breakdown

The more significant communication cost of remote work is the loss of the informal channel: the question asked in passing, the problem solved in the hallway, the thought that formed because two people happened to be in the same room at the same time. These interactions resist scheduling. They happen at the margins of the workday and in the spaces between formal meetings. Remote work eliminates the conditions that produce them naturally and replaces them with nothing, unless the organization deliberately creates substitutes. Which most do not.

The Boundary Blur

The most significant structural cost of working from home is the absence of a defined ending. The commute home was not merely transportation. It was a physical transition that signaled the workday was over and another part of life was beginning. Remote work eliminates that transition, and without a substitute the workday has no natural edge. The laptop is three feet from the bed. The phone notification at 9 PM looks identical to one at 9 AM. The result is not more work done but work occupying the psychological space of the entire waking day, producing lower output from higher exhaustion.

The Real Office Alternative

The answer is not necessarily to return to the traditional 9-to-5 model, and it is certainly not to pretend that remote work has no genuine advantages. Flexibility, reduced commuting, and better work-life integration are real benefits for a lot of people. The argument here is narrower than "remote work is bad." The argument is that when your home becomes a full-time screen environment, the same forces described throughout this book, constant connectivity, blurred boundaries, the permanent availability of digital distraction, stop being a problem you have only in your evenings and weekends. They become a problem you have all day, every day, in every room of your house.

The Choice

Working from home can be a reasonable arrangement. Working from home with no boundaries, no structure, and no physical separation from the always-on digital environment is something else. It is one continuous screen session with occasional interruptions for sleep.

The suggestions throughout this book, turning off notifications, setting deliberate time boundaries, recovering your attention from algorithms, become dramatically harder when your work requires you to be online all day in the same space where you live. That is not an argument against remote work. It is an argument for building deliberate structure around it: a defined workspace, a start time and an end time, a physical signal that work is over, and regular reasons to leave your house and exist in the physical world with other human beings.

The boundary between work and life matters for the same reason that the boundary between screen time and non-screen time matters: without it, you are always in one environment, always partially on, always available, and never fully anywhere. Your home should be a place you get to leave work. Make sure you can still do that, even if leaving work no longer means going anywhere.

Chapter 10: The Inbox That Never Empties

How Work Messaging Colonized Every Waking Hour

Congratulations. You made it all the way to Chapter 10 without anyone mentioning the thing that is probably eating more of your waking hours than television ever did. I saved it for now because people get defensive about this one. They will admit they watch too much Netflix. They will confess they scroll Instagram at 1 AM. But suggest that their relationship with work email is a problem and they will look at you like you have proposed banning oxygen. "That's WORK," they say, with the emphasis of someone who has just been accused of a crime. "I HAVE to check it." This book is about to ruin that excuse for you.

Email. Slack. Teams. The work messaging platforms that ping, buzz, and demand with the relentlessness of a slot machine, except instead of coins they dispense the feeling that you are on top of things, which turns out to be just as addictive.

The Urgency Illusion

Work messaging platforms are designed around the premise that everything is potentially urgent. The unread badge on your email app does not distinguish between a note from your CEO and a newsletter you forgot to unsubscribe from. The Slack notification sound is the same whether someone needs you immediately or someone posted a GIF in the general channel. The system treats all incoming messages as equally demanding of your attention, which means your nervous system learns to treat them the same way.

The result is a permanent background hum of low-level urgency that never fully resolves. You answer one email and two more arrive. You clear your Slack notifications and the channel reactivates thirty seconds later. There is no finishing state. The inbox that empties is a myth told to motivate people who have already given up hope. The actual experience of modern work messaging is an endless queue that shrinks and grows but never reaches zero, managed by someone who checks it compulsively because they have been trained to believe that not checking is irresponsible.

This is not productivity. This is reactive living dressed up as professional competence.

The Always-On Expectation

Somewhere in the last fifteen years, workplace culture quietly adopted a new standard: the expectation of near-instant response. Not because any policy said so. Not because anyone announced it. But because once enough people started responding to messages within minutes, the people who took hours started seeming slow, disengaged, or unavailable. The social norm shifted without a vote.

The consequence is that the workday no longer has edges. Your phone sits on the dinner table because someone might need you. You check email before you get out of bed because the overnight messages might contain something that changes your morning. You respond to a Slack message at 10 PM because the green dot is on and you have been seen. The boundary between work time and not-work time has been replaced by a continuous fog of low-level availability that exhausts people who cannot name why they are exhausted.

This is the previous chapter's problem extended: remote work did not just bring screens into your home. Work messaging brought your job into every room of your life and switched it to always-on. The television you can turn off. The Slack notification arrives whether you want it to or not.

The Shallow Work Trap

Here is what nobody tells you about managing a full inbox: it feels like working. The physical experience of reading, processing, and responding to messages is indistinguishable from the physical experience of doing actual work. You are at your desk, eyes on screen, typing. The message count is going down. By any visible measure, you are being productive.

But email management is not work. It is the logistics of work. The thinking, creating, and problem-solving that constitute genuine professional contribution require extended focus, the kind that is impossible when you are checking messages every few minutes. Every notification is a context switch. Every context switch costs mental energy and recovery time. Research on knowledge work has consistently found that interruptions cost far more time than they appear to, the minutes spent reading the message and the time needed to return to depth afterward.

The person who spends six hours managing messages and two hours doing real work does not feel underproductive. They feel exhausted. They went through all the physical motions of a full day. What they did not do was think, create, or contribute anything that required their specific expertise. They spent their professional capacity on the equivalent of filing and answering the phone.

The Status Signal Problem

Work messaging platforms have introduced a new form of social performance into professional life: the visible-activity signal. Your colleagues can see when you were last active on

Slack. Your manager can see when your email was read. The green dot next to your name is a public declaration that you are at your desk, available, and engaged.

This has created a new workplace anxiety: the fear of being seen as offline. People leave their computers running during lunch so the activity status stays green. They respond to messages immediately not because the message requires an immediate response but because they want the read receipt to show quickly. They check Slack on their phones during evenings not because anything urgent is happening but because going dark feels like a statement they are not prepared to make.

This is the social media performance dynamic, the need for visible engagement as a proxy for worth, imported directly into the workplace. The difference is that Instagram likes are optional. The professional performance of availability carries real career anxiety behind it, which makes it considerably harder to stop.

The Evening Creep

There is a specific kind of Sunday evening dread that work messaging has created: the pre-Monday inbox check. It happens around 7 or 8 PM. You tell yourself you are just looking. You just want to know what is waiting. You are "preparing." You are "being responsible." What you are doing is voluntarily extending your work week by half a day, for free, in exchange for the privilege of spending Sunday evening anxious about Monday. This is a bargain so bad that if an employer proposed it explicitly, you would laugh in their face. But you have been doing it every Sunday for years without anyone asking you to.

The email you read Sunday night will not be acted on until Monday morning. Reading it did not prepare you. It moved the worry from an unknown future problem to a known present problem, and then left you with the problem and no ability to address it for another twelve hours. You have gained nothing except the loss of Sunday evening.

I did this for years. The pre-Monday check was a ritual I had never examined. I just knew that Sunday evenings involved the laptop opening at some point and a mild anxious crawl through whatever had accumulated since Friday. It did not help. It never helped. The emails were not acted on until Monday. The reading them did not make Monday easier. It made Sunday worse. I stopped when I noticed that I felt better on the Sundays when I forgot to check, and worse on the ones when I remembered.

The evening creep is what happens when you allow the inbox to exist in personal time. Once you have established the habit of checking work messages during evenings and weekends, your brain stops treating those times as genuine rest. They become standby mode, not working, but not fully off either. Never fully anywhere.

The Fix

The solution is not to quit your job. It is to establish the same deliberate boundaries around work communications that this book advocates for entertainment screens. Turn off notifications outside of defined working hours. Check email at scheduled times rather than continuously. Set your messaging status to offline when you need focused work time and leave it there unapologetically.

These changes feel radical because the prevailing culture treats constant availability as professionalism. It is not. Constant availability is the enemy of the sustained focus that genuine professional work requires. The people doing the most important work in any field are almost never the most immediately responsive. They are the ones who have protected enough uninterrupted time to think.

Your inbox will survive two hours without you. More importantly, so will your career. If it won't, if your job genuinely requires instant availability at all hours, that is a structural problem worth addressing directly rather than accommodating indefinitely by sacrificing your evenings to a phone that never turns off. The inbox will not die of loneliness. It has never once thought about you.

Using communication skills to build

The irony of the inbox chapter is that the skill it describes, clear, direct, purposeful written communication, is among the most valuable creative assets a person can develop. The person who writes well and communicates precisely has a capability that translates directly to every contributing platform: the newsletter, the long-form article, the course, the book, the client pitch, the thread that builds an audience.

The inbox is a bad place to deploy that skill because it is reactive by design, you are responding to other people's agendas. The same skill deployed proactively produces something different: the proposal that closes the deal, the summary that saves the meeting, the documentation that means you never have to explain the same process twice. AI makes this faster. You arrive with the substance; the tool helps you communicate it clearly. That is a practical use that pays off directly in your professional life. If you also want to publish, a newsletter, a blog, something with an audience, the same skill scales. But the professional application comes first and requires no platform, no audience, and no camera.

If you find yourself spending serious time managing email, you are probably a capable communicator. That capability is wasted on inbox management. Point it at something that produces a real outcome, a cleaner process, a decision made, a document that did not exist before you wrote it. The tool is the same. The direction changes everything.

The Choice

An inbox is a tool. It should be checked when you decide to check it, on a schedule you control, and left alone the rest of the time. The work will still be there. The work does not need a babysitter.

The most productive thing you can do for your professional life is protect the time when you are not working. That time is where recovery, creativity, and perspective live. When you let the inbox eat it, you do not get more work done. You just get more tired.

Chapter 11: Netflix and No Chill

What the Streaming Default Is Doing to Your Evenings

Streaming services eliminated every friction point that used to make television a bounded activity. The fixed schedule, the seasonal break, the weekly wait between episodes, all gone. What replaced them was a genuinely infinite content environment with no natural endpoint. The default is no longer watching a show. It is being in a state of watching, indefinitely, until something external interrupts it.

Streaming platforms have turned the completion of a television series into a unit of social currency. The speed at which someone finished all available episodes is discussed in social settings as though it represents an accomplishment rather than the absence of other activities. This norm benefits the platform: binge-watching is marketed as a feature, celebrated in promotional materials, and enabled as frictionlessly as possible. A behavior that benefits the platform has been successfully packaged as a lifestyle.

The Endless Scroll of Choices

The infinite content library creates a specific psychological trap: the sense that any specific choice leaves something better unwatched. Streaming platforms have data on how much time their users spend browsing rather than watching. The browsing is not a failure state. It is engagement. The platform profits from the time spent deciding just as much as from the time spent watching.

The Attention Span Destruction

When the platform starts the next episode automatically, it trains the brain to expect narrative momentum without friction. The novel that takes three chapters to develop, the skill that takes three months to show results, the relationship that takes three years to deepen, none of these provide the immediate payoff that streaming has normalized. The attention calibration carries over.

The Social Isolation Engine

Shared viewing is not the same as connection. Two people watching the same thing are in proximity but not in exchange. Their attention is directed at the screen, not at each other. The occasional commentary, 'did you see that', is not conversation. It is synchronized consumption. Families can finish a four-hour binge and feel like they spent time together when they were simply in the same room, pointed in the same direction, for four hours. The feeling of togetherness is real. The togetherness it represents is not.

The Comparison Problem

Television has always presented idealized versions of life. What streaming has changed is the density and pacing. When a narrative resolves its central conflicts in forty-two minutes, every week, for eight seasons, it creates a cognitive template for how problems work: they are interesting, solvable, and they conclude. The actual texture of most people's lives, problems that do not resolve cleanly, relationships that require years of quiet maintenance, long stretches of nothing dramatic, compares unfavorably to that template. The template was built by writers in a room.

The Sleep Destroyer

The platform has no incentive to help you stop. Episodes end on cliffhangers. The next starts before you have decided to watch it. Every interface feature removes a natural exit point. Netflix stated publicly that their primary competitor was sleep. That is not a metaphor for ambition. It is a description of the design objective.

The Conversation Killer

Shared entertainment is a legitimate social experience. The concern is the ratio: when the primary material of social conversation is other people's fictional lives rather than your own actual ones, the conversation is doing something different from connection. It is consumption in a social wrapper, more engaging than watching alone, but not the same thing as the exchange of genuine experience.

The Creativity Killer

The more significant cost of heavy streaming consumption is not the hours. It is the cognitive state those hours produce. Watching is passive. Making something is not. The mental capacity required to start a creative project, to hold an intention, tolerate the friction of a blank page, develop something from nothing, atrophies without use. A person who spends several hours daily in passive reception is not resting that capacity. They are allowing it to weaken by substituting consumption for the activity that would maintain it.

The Reality Check

There is no upper limit on the content available to consume. More is being produced constantly, faster than any individual could watch. The 'keeping up' feeling that streaming culture generates has no resolution: you are not falling behind because there is nothing to be ahead of. The industry has designed the feeling of being behind because that feeling keeps you watching. The correct response to an infinite feed is not to consume more of it. It is to stop treating it as a queue with an end.

The Alternative

The question is not whether to watch anything. It is whether the watching is something you chose or something that happened by default. A show watched deliberately, because you wanted to see it, for a defined period, turned off when it ends, is a different activity from the autoplay that runs because stopping requires a decision. The first is entertainment. The second is the platform running your evening for you. Both look identical from the outside. They are not the same experience.

What intentional watching looks like

None of this means streaming is worthless. Great television exists. Documentaries teach. Films expand imagination. The problem is not the content. It is the default. Binge-watching as a lifestyle is different from watching a specific thing because you chose to watch it.

The contributing side of streaming is modest but real: watch things that feed work you are doing, conversations you are having, or skills you are building. Watch with intention and stop when the intended thing is done. The autoplay is not your schedule. You are.

If you produce anything, writing, teaching, creative work, consuming good creative work is part of the job. The distinction is between watching as a deliberate act of learning or enjoyment and watching as a default for any hour that does not have another plan.

Every hour of content on every streaming platform was made by someone who was not watching it. Writers, directors, composers, editors, all of them sat down in the hours that most people spend on the consuming side and produced the thing you are consuming. The contributing side of streaming is the person who makes something people put on a list. Not the person who maintains the list.

Chapter 12: When Your Highest Achievement is a Digital Badge

What Digital Achievement Systems Are Built to Do

Gaming has become one of the largest entertainment industries on earth, larger than film and music combined. It has achieved this by solving a problem every other entertainment medium has struggled with: how to make the user feel genuinely accomplished rather than merely entertained. The solution was achievement systems, and those systems are the subject of this chapter.

The Achievement Trap

Modern games are built around achievement systems that map precisely onto the reward mechanisms behavioral psychology has identified as most effective at producing compulsive engagement. Every action earns points. Every task completion unlocks something. Every level crossed produces a visible acknowledgment of progress. These systems are not incidental. They are the primary engineering challenge the designers are solving: how to keep the player in a state where the next reward feels close enough to justify continued play. The result is a medium that delivers the sensation of accomplishment at a frequency that no other domain in life matches. Which is a problem when the accomplishment does not transfer outside the game.

The Time Vampire

The hours involved in heavy gaming are substantial. The average self-described serious gamer reports roughly six hours of daily play, 42 hours per week, more than a full-time job.

Unlike a full-time job, it produces no external output and develops no capability that transfers to anything outside the specific game being played. The time cost is real. The absence of accumulated value from that time becomes visible only when the person tries to account for what several years of heavy gaming has produced.

The Social Isolation Chamber

Online multiplayer gaming provides social experience that is real but narrow. The collaboration is genuine within the context of the game. The relationships that develop are real within the limits of the platform. The problem is not that these connections are fake. It is that they are contextual in a way that face-to-face relationships are not: they exist inside the game environment, depend on continued participation in it, and do not produce the kind of embedded knowledge of another person, their life circumstances, their struggles, their history outside the game, that close friendship requires.

The Skill Transfer Problem

Gaming does develop certain skills: pattern recognition, spatial reasoning, rapid decision-making. The limitation is transfer. These capacities are highly specific to the game environment and do not compound the way skills developed through real-world application do. The person who has spent 5,000 hours becoming expert at a specific game has developed mastery of a closed system, not 5,000 hours of transferable capability.

The Reality Comparison Problem

Real life operates on slower timelines with ambiguous feedback and no progress bar. Games are engineered with the opposite: instant rewards, visible progress, clear objectives. The calibration problem is not that games are unrealistically rewarding. It is that the brain adapts to the calibration. After extended exposure to gaming reward schedules, the natural pace of real-world progress begins to register as unreasonably slow rather than simply as how things work.

The Financial Drain

Gaming has become expensive in ways that aren't obvious. The initial purchase is just the entry fee. Expansion packs, downloadable content, microtransactions, subscription passes, and hardware upgrade pressure create an ongoing cost that most players never add up. Many games now include in-game purchases for virtual items, cosmetic upgrades, character skins, advantage boosts, that exist only within that specific game and disappear entirely when the servers shut down. You are paying real money for things that will cease to exist on a timeline you do not control.

The body keeps a separate ledger. Back tight, eyes dry, sleep disrupted, weight trending upward. The virtual achievements feel urgent in a way that physical health does not, until the physical health becomes impossible to ignore.

I do not game. My stepson does. I have watched him develop the specific posture this implies, the shoulders, the squint, the complete dislocation from whatever else is happening in the room, and I have watched him notice none of it. That is the tell. The person who has lost track of their body is usually also the person who has lost track of the clock.

The Real World Alternative

The test for whether gaming is a leisure activity or a default substitution is not the number of hours. It is what the hours are displacing. Physical health, close relationships, skill development, financial stability, these compound over time in a way that gaming does not. A person who games in the hours that belong to those things is not resting. They are substituting a closed-system reward for an open-system one. The closed system is always easier. The open system is the one that builds a life.

The Choice

The test is simple: at the end of a year of gaming, what exists that did not exist before? The virtual achievements do not transfer. The rank does not compound. The relationships formed inside the game context do not persist when the context disappears. The closed system is always more immediately satisfying than the open one, which is why the substitution is so reliable and so costly. Open-system accomplishment, skills that build, relationships that deepen, work that accumulates, is the version that exists outside the server.

When gaming becomes something more

Gaming does have a contributing side, and it is worth naming. Game development is a legitimate and growing creative field that begins with the same hours most gamers spend consuming. Tools like Unity and Godot are free. Communities for learning are vast and active. The person who redirects even a fraction of gaming time toward building games rather than playing them is developing skills that transfer: programming, design thinking, problem-solving under constraint. But the redirect does not have to be game development. It can be any skill that produces something cumulative in the hours gaming currently occupies. The point is not what replaces the gaming. The point is that something does.

Streaming gaming content is also a real creative economy, though it is worth being honest that it rewards a small number of entertainers and functions primarily as passive consumption for everyone watching. The question is always which side of the camera you are on.

The gaming skills themselves, pattern recognition, spatial reasoning, rapid decision-making under pressure, are real. The question is whether they are being applied to anything that exists outside the game. If the answer is no, the chapter above is the honest accounting.

Gaming as an industry is larger than film and music combined. Every dollar of it was built by people who were on the contributing side, designing systems, writing code, building worlds, documenting culture. The contributing side of gaming is the developer, the modder, the streamer building an audience, the writer who covers it. The hours are the same. The direction is different.

Chapter 13: The House Always Wins

How Sports Betting Apps Turned Your Phone into a Casino That Never Closes

Let me describe something that would have sounded insane in 2015: you are lying in bed at 11 PM, and with four taps on your phone you can place a real-money bet on whether the next pitch in a minor league baseball game in Albuquerque will be a ball or a strike. No cash, no trip to a casino, no standing in line at a sportsbook. Four taps. Done. This is not a hypothetical. This is Tuesday.

In 2018, the United States Supreme Court struck down a federal ban on sports betting, and the gambling industry moved with a speed that regulators, researchers, and the public were not prepared for. Within seven years, 38 states plus Washington D.C. Had legalized sports betting. Thirty of those states allow online and mobile betting. You can now open an app on your phone and place a wager on a baseball game, a tennis match, the next pitch, the next serve, or whether a specific player will record a particular statistical outcome in the next five minutes. The whole transaction takes about as long as sending a text message. No cash, no casino, no trip anywhere. The barrier between impulse and bet has been reduced to a few taps on a screen.

The American Gaming Association reports that Americans have wagered more than a quarter of a trillion dollars on sports betting since the Supreme Court ruling, that is more than the GDP of Greece, and 94% of those bets were placed online.

As of 2025, roughly 48% of American men between 18 and 49 report having at least one sportsbook account (American Gaming Association, 2025). Not 48% of gamblers. 48% of men. Nearly half. This chapter is not a coincidence. The gambling industry spent decades lobbying for exactly this access. When it arrived, the industry was ready. The regulators, the researchers, and the public were not.

The Same Machine, Different Name

Here is the thing about FanDuel and DraftKings that the commercials featuring famous comedians and retired athletes do not mention: the people who built these apps spent years studying exactly what makes slot machines addictive, and then they made a slot machine you can carry in your pocket. The sports betting companies have learned everything from Silicon Valley. Their apps are engineered using the same behavioral psychology that powers social media, variable reward schedules, push notifications, personalized offers timed to moments of maximum vulnerability, and algorithmic targeting of users who show signs of compulsive behavior. A former FanDuel employee described the company's approach to users under 25 this way: "Those are the guys that bring you all the money." The companies have identified that young men who are heavy users are the most valuable segment, and they have designed their products accordingly.

The product has also been designed to maximize the speed and frequency of betting. Today, 90% of bets are placed on phones, and more than half are live in-game bets placed while the game is in progress. The apps offer what the industry calls "microbetting", wagers on individual plays, pitches, and possessions that resolve in seconds and immediately present the next opportunity. The feedback loop between bet, outcome, and next bet has been compressed to the point where it operates more like a slot machine than a sportsbook. The options are literally limitless: on any given NFL Sunday, a user can bet on a qualifying tennis match between two players ranked outside the top 100 in Charlottesville, Virginia. Not because anyone is a tennis fan. Because someone wants more action, and the app is designed to provide it continuously.

The Scale of the Problem

The National Council on Problem Gambling estimates that when sports betting is conducted on phones and computers, the rate of disordered gambling reaches as high as 16%, with another 13% of online bettors showing signs of compulsive behavior without yet meeting the clinical threshold. Roughly 30% of online sports bettors show some form of gambling problem. This is at minimum twice the rate found among gamblers in general.

Since legalization, searches for help with gambling addiction have jumped 23% nationally, and in some early-legalizing states like Massachusetts, Pennsylvania, and Ohio, the increase approached or surpassed 50%. Gamblers Anonymous chapters are getting younger: one meeting coordinator in Massachusetts reported that two-thirds of the 17 new members who joined in five months were in their 20s or 30s, and all of them had come because of sports betting apps.

The economic distribution of losses is concentrated in a small group that the companies actively grow. A 2024 study of 700,000 online sports bettors (published in Nature Human Behaviour) found that 3% of them generated more than 50% of sportsbook revenue. A study of 9 million bettors from the 2023-2024 NFL season found that 60% of bettors accounted for just 1% of revenue. The companies are profitable because they have identified and retained the heaviest users, and they are exceptionally good at identifying who those users are before those users are aware of it themselves.

The Johns Hopkins Bloomberg School of Public Health called it "the largest and fastest explosion of gambling the country has ever seen." Gambling disorder, recognized in the

DSM-5 in the same category as substance use disorders, carries a higher suicide risk than most other addiction disorders. One in five people with a gambling disorder attempt or complete suicide. There is no federal funding for gambling addiction research. The treatment system is almost entirely state-based and dramatically underfunded relative to the problem.

The Hidden Addiction

Gambling is called the hidden addiction for a reason, and the phone has made it more hidden than ever. There is no smell. There is no slurred speech. There is no physical change. A person can be gambling hundreds of times a day, stepping away during dinner, betting at 2 AM on a Taiwanese basketball game, placing 500 wagers in a single day on live microbets, and nobody in their life will see it happening. The phone is always in their hand anyway. That is the point. The excuse is always plausible. The losses are invisible until the bank account is empty or the credit card bills arrive.

The concealment compounds the harm. A person with a drinking problem is at some point visibly drunk. A person with a gambling problem can be a functioning professional during the day and a person in crisis at 3 AM, and the two versions of their life are completely invisible to each other until one of them destroys the other. A psychiatrist profiled by the Wall Street Journal in 2024 knew the neuroscience of addiction, tried to self-exclude from DraftKings, and still lost over $400,000 before stopping. She described becoming "a mystery to herself." This is not a failure of willpower. This is a product designed by people who understand addiction science better than most of their users do.

I have known people who developed gambling problems before smartphone betting existed, the kind that required a trip to a casino or a call to a bookie. What strikes me about the mobile version is how the concealment works differently. The old version was visible in the absences: the guy who disappeared on weekends, the money that could not be accounted for. The phone version hides inside behavior that looks completely normal. Everyone is on their phone. There is no absence to notice.

The Normalization Machine

The broadcast saturation has been deliberate and effective. Roughly 5% of in-game NFL advertisements are for sports gambling. ESPN launched its own sportsbook. The halftime show now includes betting odds coverage. Celebrities, athletes, and comedians appear in ads that glamorize betting the way cigarette ads once glamorized smoking. The Rutgers University gambling research director drew exactly that comparison: "Gambling is where cigarettes were in the '40s, when we had the Marlboro Man and every actress with a cigarette. Right now it's glamorized. People are not understanding that this is an addiction like any other."

A 2025 survey found 86% of online sports bettors believed they could reliably make money betting on sports. Among bettors aged 18 to 34, it was 82%. The apps are winning in part because they have successfully convinced the majority of their users that the house does not have an overwhelming mathematical advantage, an advantage that is the foundational fact of how the business works.

Where the analytical instinct pays off

Sports betting is one of the few domains in this book where the contributing side is thin enough to require honesty rather than optimism. There is no version of mobile microbetting that builds something. The product is engineered to consume money and time, and the house's mathematical advantage ensures that the analytical instinct, the feeling that you can read a game, identify value, outsmart the line, is precisely what the platform is designed to exploit.

The analytical instinct itself, however, is real and transferable. The person who is drawn to sports betting because they enjoy statistical analysis and competitive prediction has a genuine capability that can be directed elsewhere. Financial markets reward the same skills applied to actual assets that you own and that can compound over time. Sports analytics as a career field is real and growing. Building a model, a system, or a research practice in any domain where your edge can accumulate, rather than a casino where it cannot, is the redirect the instinct deserves.

The honest version of the contributing side here is not 'use betting platforms differently.' It is 'the competitive and analytical energy that makes betting feel compelling belongs somewhere it can build something.'

The Choice

Most people who bet on sports will not develop a gambling disorder. Most casual bettors lose small amounts and treat it as entertainment. This book is not arguing that everyone who places a Super Bowl wager is one step from financial ruin. The argument is narrower: that a specific type of product, the mobile microbetting app with algorithmic targeting and 24/7 availability, has been deliberately designed to function as close to a slot machine as sports betting law allows, and that it is operating at a scale and with a level of advertising saturation that makes it impossible for many users to correctly assess the risk before the habit is established.

The same question that applies to every other chapter in this book applies here: is this tool serving you, or are you serving it? If you open the betting app because you enjoy a specific wager on a specific game and you would do the same thing with the same composure whether you won or lost, it is probably entertainment. If you open it compulsively, if you bet on events you have no interest in because you need the action, if you find yourself checking it during dinner or lying about how much time you spend on it, that is the product working as designed, on a user it was designed to find.

The house always wins in aggregate. It can afford to let you win sometimes. The winning is the product. The winning is what keeps you in the app. There is no version of this where you beat the algorithm over time. The algorithm has your data, your history, your pattern, and an unlimited bankroll. You have your phone and the feeling that your luck is about to change. It is not about to change. The contributing side of the sports betting economy is the person who built the app.

Chapter 14: Instagram Travel Doesn't Count as Going Places

And Other Lies We Tell Ourselves About Virtual Experiences

Digital platforms have created a new category of substitution that is more insidious than outright passive consumption: the consumption of content about activities as a substitute for the activities themselves. Watching travel videos is not traveling. Following fitness accounts is not exercising. Bookmarking recipes is not cooking. These are all forms of engagement that feel like participation because they involve the same subject matter, while systematically avoiding the friction that actual participation requires.

The friction is the point. The discomfort of getting on a plane, the physical demand of a workout, the failure of a first attempt at a recipe: these are not obstacles between you and the experience. They are the experience. They are what makes the thing stick. The curated version excludes them by design, which is why the curated version is easier to consume and why it produces nothing in the person who consumes it.

What Vicarious Experience Actually Provides

There is a genuine use for content about activities: it can function as preparation, inspiration, or research for the actual thing. Travel videos can help you choose where to go and what to do when you get there. Cooking videos can give you techniques to practice. Fitness content can introduce you to movements you have not tried.

The problem is not the content. It is the substitution. When content about an activity consistently replaces the activity rather than preceding it, you have created a loop that provides the feeling of engagement with the subject while preventing the development of any real relationship with it. The person who has watched a hundred cooking videos without cooking has not learned to cook. They have developed a relationship with watching cooking videos, which is a completely different thing.

The Competence Illusion

Content consumption about a subject creates a false sense of familiarity with it. The person who has watched documentaries about mountaineering knows the vocabulary, recognizes the landmarks, and can discuss the subject with apparent confidence. They have not developed the physical capability, the judgment under pressure, or the embodied knowledge that comes from climbing. The confidence gap between what they know and what they can do is real and potentially dangerous, but it is invisible to them because nothing has tested it.

I once spent an evening watching travel videos about Portugal, the light in Lisbon, the tiles on the buildings, the food markets in Porto. It was beautiful. It was also nothing. Two years later I went to Portugal. The cobblestones hurt my feet. I got lost twice. I ordered something I couldn't pronounce and it turned out to be the best meal of the trip. None of that, the discomfort, the lostness, the lucky accident, existed in the videos. The videos had curated it out. That is precisely why the videos are not the same as going.

The Choice

The friction that travel, cooking, and physical activity require is not a design flaw. It is the mechanism by which the experience becomes yours. The discomfort, the failure, the lucky accident, none of it exists in the curated version. None of it can.

The contributing side of experience is showing up for the real thing, including its costs.

Consuming someone else's experience of a place is not the same as going there. The difference is not abstract. It is sensory, physical, unpredictable, and impossible to curate. A walk somewhere you have never been costs more than scrolling photos of it. That cost is why it sticks.

Chapter 15: The YouTube Rabbit Hole

Where Two Hours of Your Life Goes When You Click on One Video

YouTube is the largest video platform on earth and one of the most effective attention capture systems ever built. Over a billion hours of video are watched on it every day. The platform is powered by a recommendation algorithm that does not optimize for quality, accuracy, or user satisfaction. It optimizes for continued watching. These are not the same objective, and the gap between them is where most of the platform's damage is done.

The mechanism is familiar from the rest of this book: variable reward, emotional arousal, and the elimination of natural stopping points. The autoplay that starts the next video, the thumbnail designed to trigger anxiety or excitement, the recommendation that surfaces content slightly more extreme than the last one, all of this is the same engineering applied to a different format. The format here is longer, which means the session length is longer and the relationship between the creator and the viewer has more time to develop into something that feels like trust.

The Thumbnail as Promise

YouTube thumbnails are a distinct cultural artifact: a form of visual communication whose sole purpose is to induce a click. The open mouth, the pointing finger, the all-caps text promising revelation, these conventions developed because they work. They trigger the same curiosity and anxiety loops that make news notifications hard to ignore. Every thumbnail is a small act of deception: it promises significance that the content rarely delivers, and the viewer clicks anyway because the promise is compelling and the cost of clicking is nothing.

After years of training on this format, the brain adapts. Content that does not open with immediate emotional payoff gets abandoned in the first thirty seconds. The platform has data on this and creators respond accordingly, front-loading every video with the most dramatic moment and eliminating any second that might lose the viewer. The result is a medium that has trained its audience to be incapable of the sustained attention the medium itself no longer provides.

The Long-Form Credibility Machine

YouTube has a fake expertise problem that is distinct from every other platform's fake expertise problem, because YouTube has the time to make you genuinely believe someone. A fifteen-second TikTok cannot build much credibility. But a forty-five-minute video, produced weekly for three years, with a custom intro, branded graphics, consistent production quality, and a presenter who knows how to hold a camera and speak to it like a trusted friend, that can build real authority with an audience, regardless of whether the underlying knowledge is real.

The platform is full of people who have turned their autodidactic hobby into a credential. The person with 800,000 subscribers who has been making videos about nutrition for four years feels like an expert because they present like an expert. The production values signal competence. The comment section, full of people saying their advice worked, provides social proof. The sheer volume of content creates the impression of depth. None of this is evidence of expertise. It is evidence of consistency and camera comfort.

Real expertise is built through years of study, failure, peer review, and practice that nobody watches. YouTube expertise is built through years of posting, during which the presenter and the audience both gradually confuse familiarity with authority. By the time the presenter says something genuinely incorrect, which they will, the audience's trust has been earned through volume rather than verified through scrutiny.

This is the long-form version of misinformation: slow, confident, and trusted. It is harder to spot than a thirty-second claim because it comes wrapped in two hours of content that was mostly accurate.

The Radicalization Pipeline

The recommendation algorithm surfaces increasingly extreme content because extreme content generates stronger emotional responses and higher engagement. A viewer watching a documentary gets recommended videos questioning it. A viewer interested in nutrition gets led toward content attributing disease to deliberate poisoning. The algorithm is not promoting conspiracy. It is promoting engagement, and conspiracy content produces reliable engagement.

The Meta-Consumption Layer

Reaction content, videos of people watching other videos, responding to other people's responses, or commenting on commentary, adds another layer of mediation between the viewer and any direct experience of anything. The original content is the pretext. The reactor's responses are the product. Each layer of reaction adds another creator's attention as a buffer between you and the source material, which has now been digested twice before it reaches you. The format requires nothing from creator or viewer except continued presence. Which is precisely what the algorithm needs.

The Productivity Content Trap

The self-improvement content category on YouTube is the platform's most refined trap: content that produces the feeling of having addressed a problem while ensuring the problem continues. Watching a video about focus requires no focus. Watching a video about building discipline requires no discipline. The platform has discovered that the audience for 'how to stop wasting time' content is, by definition, people who are currently wasting time, and that the content reliably sends them to the next recommended video rather than to the activity they were watching to learn how to do.

The Parasocial Relationship Trap

The parasocial relationship that develops through YouTube is more durable than the one that develops through shorter-form platforms, because the long-form format has time to build it. A presenter who has been in your earbuds for forty-five minutes weekly for three years has accumulated the kind of presence that real friendship requires, except the relationship is entirely one-directional. The creator knows nothing about you. You know a great deal about them. The emotional investment is real; the reciprocity is not. The hours given to a creator's life are hours not given to anyone who knows you exist.

The Attention Span Destruction

YouTube has done something television never managed: it has made ten-minute videos feel slow. The platform's evolution toward Shorts, fifteen-to-sixty-second vertical clips competing directly with TikTok, reveals exactly what the algorithm has learned about its users. Longer content gets abandoned in the first thirty seconds unless it delivers a compelling hook immediately. Creators have responded by front-loading every video with the most dramatic moment, cutting ruthlessly between shots, and eliminating any second that might lose the viewer. After a year of training your attention on this format, sitting through a two-hour movie, let alone reading a book, requires the kind of willpower most people reserve for dieting.

The Engineered Session

Autoplay, the recommendation sidebar, the end-screen redirect, every feature of the interface is designed to extend the session by removing the decision to continue watching. The platform has studied where viewers leave and systematically eliminated those exit points. The conscious decision to stop is structurally harder than the unconscious decision to continue. You have to actively close the app. The platform never suggests you should.

The Learning Illusion

The platform contains genuinely educational content. The problem is that watching educational content produces the sensation of learning without the cognitive work that actual learning requires. Familiarity with information is not competence with a subject. The gap between what you have watched and what you can do is invisible until something tests it.

The Platform Pressure on Creators

The algorithm rewards upload frequency regardless of quality, penalizing creators for the time required to make something genuinely good. This creates a dependency risk on the contributing side that mirrors the consuming side: the creator who builds their entire practice around platform-optimized output gradually loses the work habits that produce anything worth watching. The contributing side of YouTube is real, but the platform applies the same pressure on creators that it applies on viewers, toward volume, speed, and the metrics that measure neither. The creator who treats the platform as a distribution channel for work developed by their own standard, rather than as the environment in which the work gets made, is the one who builds something that outlasts the algorithm's current preferences.

The Real Cost

The average YouTube user spends over forty minutes per day on the platform. That doesn't sound catastrophic until you remember that forty minutes daily is 243 hours per year, six work weeks, spent watching content that, by the platform's own data, delivers very little lasting satisfaction. The people most likely to describe themselves as "just taking a break" when they open YouTube are often the same people who open it at 9 PM and close it at midnight, genuinely unsure where the time went.

I have been one of those people. Not with YouTube specifically, my default platform was different, but I know the experience of opening something for five minutes and emerging two hours later with no satisfying account of where the time went. The platform did not take it from me. I gave it incrementally, each click extending the session by another small increment, none of which felt like a decision.

YouTube consumption creates the sensation of productivity without producing anything. The session ends and nothing exists that did not exist before it. That is the platform doing exactly what it was designed to do.

The Exit Strategy

The exit from passive YouTube consumption is not to delete the app. The app is not the problem. The default is the problem, the automatic reach, the infinite scroll, the two hours that evaporated while the algorithm served you what it knew you would not quite be satisfied by but would not quite stop watching.

The practical move is the one this book has described throughout: use it on purpose. Open it with a specific video or channel in mind. Watch that thing. Close it when it is done. Do not follow the recommendations after. This requires friction you have to add yourself, because the platform removes every natural stopping point by design. Add the friction deliberately. The autoplay is not your schedule. You are.

If the habit is too entrenched for moderation to work, removal is a legitimate reset, not as a permanent ideology, but as a break. A month without the app breaks the automatic reach. After the month, reinstall it as a tool rather than a default. The goal is a purposeful relationship with the platform, not an abstinent one.

YouTube as a creator platform

YouTube is also the largest free educational infrastructure ever built and one of the most accessible paths to audience-building available to anyone with expertise and something to say. The same recommendation algorithm described in this chapter that traps viewers in rabbit holes is also surfacing the right video to the right person at precisely the right moment, if someone is making the right video.

Teaching on YouTube has produced doctors, lawyers, engineers, chefs, musicians, and craftspeople who built substantial audiences and real income by documenting what they already knew. The barrier to entry is a phone, something worth saying, and the willingness to be bad at it for a while. The consuming side of YouTube is infinite and engineered for passivity. The contributing side is one of the more genuine opportunities available to anyone with knowledge and the willingness to share it.

If you have expertise, in anything, there is an audience for it. The people currently watching mediocre videos about your subject are there because nobody has made the good version yet. The algorithm will surface your content if it is genuinely useful. It is the one case where the algorithm is working for you rather than against you.

The Choice

The choice is not between YouTube and nothing. It is between YouTube as a default that runs in place of your own time and YouTube as a tool you use when it serves a specific purpose. The first relationship produces the sessions that end at midnight with no satisfying account of where the evening went. The second produces the research completed, the skill introduced, the specific thing watched and then stopped.

The algorithm will always be there if you want it. But here is the thing about YouTube specifically: it is very good at making you feel like you accomplished something when you didn't. You watched twelve videos, learned some facts, followed some interesting threads, and ended up exactly where you started, except two hours older. That feeling of productive consumption is the platform's most effective trick. The only counter to it is doing something that produces an actual result: a page written, a meal cooked, a conversation had, a skill practiced. Something the algorithm cannot take credit for.

Chapter 16: The Machine That Thinks For You

What AI Tools Are Doing to Your Ability to Think

What I am going to tell you is what I have noticed about how people, including, at times, myself, use AI tools in daily life, which is almost nothing like the careful, deliberate use the technology is capable of supporting. Most people do not use AI to enhance their thinking. They use it to replace their thinking. And that is a very different thing.

The Instant Answer Trap

There was a time when finding information required you to do something. You typed words into a search engine, looked at the results, clicked on a few, read them, compared them, formed a view. The whole process took maybe five minutes and resulted in you knowing something. For anyone who remembers it, that process now feels quaint. For anyone who does not, it is worth describing because the thing that replaced it works differently in ways that matter.

AI chatbots eliminate that friction entirely. You type a question in natural language and receive a confident, well-written, authoritative-sounding answer within seconds. There is nothing to evaluate, no sources to compare, no uncertainty to sit with. The answer arrives pre-digested. Your job is just to accept it.

This sounds like pure efficiency. It is, for certain tasks. If you need to know the capital of Burkina Faso or the formula for compound interest, frictionless answers are fine. The problem arises when frictionless answers start replacing the process of thinking through questions that genuinely require thought, ethical dilemmas, strategic decisions, creative problems, interpersonal situations. When you outsource those to a machine, you do not get a faster version of your own thinking. You get a statistical composite of how the internet has previously discussed similar questions. That is not the same thing.

The New Dependency

Here is what I noticed in myself about eighteen months into using these tools heavily: I started opening the chat window before I had figured out what I was trying to say. Not to research, not to edit, not to fact-check, but to think. The blank page had become uncomfortable in a new way, and the solution I had trained myself to reach for was a chatbot instead of a notebook. That is when I started paying attention.

This is the same dynamic as every other tool in this book: it begins as useful and becomes compulsive. The difference is that AI dependency has a specific cognitive cost that television and social media do not. When you outsource your thinking to an algorithm repeatedly, the mental muscle you are not using starts to atrophy. The ability to tolerate the discomfort of not yet knowing the answer, to hold a problem open while your brain works on it, to generate original ideas from scratch, these are skills. They require practice. They weaken without it.

A necessary distinction: for people with anxiety disorders, the compulsive phone-checking described in this chapter is not always a habit. It is sometimes self-medication. The phone provides a reliable source of low-effort stimulation that temporarily dampens the anxiety signal, which is why it feels so hard to put down when the anxiety is high. The advice in this chapter still applies, but if the pattern is driven by clinical anxiety rather than boredom or habit, a therapist should be part of the picture alongside any changes to screen behavior. Treating the screen use without treating the anxiety underneath it is treating the symptom while the cause keeps running.

I noticed this in my own work. I write for a living. When I started using AI tools heavily, I found my first-draft thinking getting lazier, reaching for the tool earlier in the process, before I had genuinely wrestled with what I wanted to say. The drafts were faster. They were also, initially, worse, because the tool was generating ideas rather than refining mine. The best use I have found for AI in writing is after I know what I think, as an editor, a researcher, a sounding board. Used before that point, it replaces thinking rather than supporting it.

The Confidence Problem

AI tools present information with a consistent, confident, authoritative tone regardless of whether they are correct. This is not a bug that will be fixed in the next version. It is a fundamental characteristic of how these systems work: they generate plausible-sounding text. Plausible-sounding and accurate are not the same thing. They are very hard to tell apart when the prose is fluent and you are reading fast.

The YouTube chapter discussed how long-form content builds false credibility through volume and production quality. AI has compressed this process to seconds. You can receive a fluent, detailed, well-organized explanation of something that is factually wrong before you have had time to wonder whether you should verify it. The confidence of the presentation bypasses the skepticism you would normally apply.

The people most at risk here are not the naive or the uncritical. They are busy, capable people who have learned to trust their tools and who have neither the time nor the inclination to fact-check every output. In high-stakes contexts, medical decisions, legal questions, financial choices, AI-generated confidence without AI-verified accuracy is a genuinely dangerous combination.

The Relationship Replacement

Something unexpected has emerged among heavy AI users: people forming what feel like genuine relationships with AI chatbots. They talk to them about personal problems, seek emotional support, confide fears and frustrations. The chatbot responds with empathy, asks thoughtful follow-up questions, and never judges, criticizes, or becomes unavailable. It is the perfect listener.

This is the parasocial relationship dynamic from the social media chapters, compressed into a single interface that responds directly to you. The chatbot is not your friend. It has no memory of your previous conversations unless the platform implements memory features. It has no stake in your wellbeing. It generates responses that sound caring because it has been trained on human text that includes caring responses. The feeling of being understood is real. The understanding is not.

Every hour spent processing your feelings with an AI is an hour not spent developing the skill of processing them with real people, who are messier, less available, more likely to say uncomfortable things, and vastly more valuable to your actual life. The romantic companion app category, Replika, Character.AI, and dozens of competitors, represents this dynamic at its most concentrated. That territory is covered in Chapter 22, in the context of where dating apps were always heading. The short version: 220 million downloads, $221 million in consumer spending through mid-2025, and users who have reported genuine grief when the company updated its software and changed how their AI companion behaved. Worth reading alongside this chapter.

How to Use AI Without Losing Your Mind

AI tools are genuinely useful when used deliberately, for specific tasks, after you have done your own thinking. Research, editing, summarizing, generating options you then evaluate critically, automating repetitive work: these are legitimate uses that amplify human capability rather than replacing it.

The discipline required is the same discipline required everywhere in this book: use the tool when it serves your purpose, and put it down when you are reaching for it out of habit or avoidance. Before you open the chat window, ask yourself what you are trying to do and whether thinking through it yourself first would serve you better. Often it would. Often the discomfort of not immediately having an answer is exactly the productive discomfort that leads somewhere worth going.

The test I use: would I be embarrassed if someone knew I had used AI for this? If the answer is yes, if this is something where my own thinking, judgment, or creativity is the point, I close the window and do it myself. If the answer is no, if this is logistics, research, editing, or a task where the output matters more than the process, the tool is appropriate.

Using AI on the right side of the line

Chapter 2 of this book draws a line through every digital platform. AI is where that line matters most, because the distance between the two sides is greatest. On the consuming side, AI replaces your thinking. On the contributing side, it amplifies it. The difference is not visible from the outside, both produce text. The difference is whether you are the author of what comes out.

The productive relationship with AI tools starts with your own thinking and uses the tool to extend it. You arrive with the expertise, the judgment, the specific voice, and the ideas. The AI helps you research faster, draft more fluidly, edit more rigorously, and reach further than you could alone. The output is unmistakably yours because the thinking is yours. The tool is downstream of your judgment, not upstream of it.

Practically: write your own outline before asking AI to help you develop it. Form your own opinion before asking AI to research the supporting evidence. Know what you want to say before using AI to help you say it better. In each case, you remain the author. The sequence, your thinking first, AI amplification second, is the entire difference between using AI productively and using it as an elaborate form of passivity.

AI used this way is a multiplier. You remain the thing being multiplied. The creative advantage available to a person with genuine expertise and command of these tools has no historical parallel. If you are on the contributing side of the line, this technology is the most significant creative opportunity of your working lifetime. That is not an exaggeration. It is arithmetic applied to a thousand recovered hours a year.

The Choice

AI tools will keep getting better. They will become more capable, more convincing, more useful, and more tempting to defer to. The question is not whether to use them, most people reading this book will use them, and sensibly so. The question is whether you use them as an extension of your thinking or as a substitute for it.

Your ability to think, to wrestle with hard problems, tolerate uncertainty, generate original ideas, and reason from evidence to conclusions, is not a feature that will become obsolete. It is what makes you valuable, interesting, and capable of living a life that is genuinely yours. A machine can generate text. It cannot live your life, make your decisions, or be responsible for who you become.

Keep that part for yourself.

The question of where AI dependency leads at scale, for individual users and for human cognitive capacity broadly, is the subject of two companion volumes in this series. The Death of Thinking examines what happens when AI replaces thinking at population level over time. The Birth of the Augmented Human examines the alternative: what the contributing side of AI makes possible when the tools are used to extend genuine human capability rather than substitute for it. Both futures are real possibilities. Which one materializes depends on the accumulated choices of people like the ones reading this chapter.

The fourth volume in the series, Stuck in the Middle, examines what happens to the people caught between those two futures, the ones who did not choose a side and got sorted by default. A companion volume, The Enshittification of America, examines the broader pattern of platform degradation, the systematic process by which services that once worked for their users are redesigned to extract maximum value from them instead. The pattern described in that book is the economic infrastructure underneath everything this chapter has named about AI: the same forces that turned social media from a connection tool into an attention farm are already at work on AI platforms.

Chapter 17: The Podcast That Ate Your Walk

Why Passive Audio Consumption Is Still Passive Consumption

This book has told you, in several places, to take walks. Go outside. Leave the screen behind. Move your body through the physical world without a destination or an agenda. Good advice. Solid advice. Advice that many readers will immediately translate into: "Take walks with podcasts."

I listen to podcasts. Some of the best long-form conversation happening anywhere is happening in podcast format. This is not a case against podcasts. It is a case against using them to fill every available silence, a habit I had to consciously break and one that is worth examining if you recognize it in yourself.

But podcasts during walks are not two birds with one stone. They are one bird with no stone. You are walking and listening, which means you are not really doing either. You are moving your body while someone else occupies your mind. The walk, which was supposed to give your brain space to breathe, has become another content delivery session.

The Boredom Problem

Chapter 27 of this book makes the case for productive boredom, the creative, restorative, insight-generating mental state that only emerges when your mind is not occupied with external input. The walk without earbuds is one of the most reliable ways to access that state. You are moving your body, which activates thinking. You are not consuming content, which clears space for original thought. Many people's best ideas arrive on walks. Not because walking is magic, but because it is one of the few times in modern life when the mind is both active and unoccupied.

Plug in a podcast and that window closes. Your mind is occupied. The creative idling that produces insight has been replaced by passive reception. You will finish the walk knowing what the podcast hosts think about something. You will not have thought about anything yourself. This is fine occasionally. As a default, it is a way of being continuously entertained while calling it a walk.

The Productivity Disguise

Podcasts are the most socially acceptable form of passive consumption because they are not visually associated with sloth. Lying on a couch watching Netflix carries cultural baggage. Walking while listening to a podcast about history, business, or current events carries none. You look productive. You feel productive. You can tell people about it: "I've been listening to this great podcast about ancient Rome."

But the cognitive experience is structurally similar to television. You are receiving content created by someone else, processed passively, retained at about the same rate as anything you watch rather than read or actively engage with. The main difference is that your legs are moving.

This matters because podcasts have also colonized the last remaining silence in daily life. The commute that used to be a transition space, a decompression chamber between work and home, is now filled with content. The exercise that used to be physical and mental downtime now has a soundtrack. The cooking, the cleaning, the waiting, every ambient task that previously gave the brain unstructured time has been claimed by audio consumption. There is no silence left in which an unprompted thought might form.

The Case For Podcasts

Podcasts are not inherently bad. At their best, they are long-form conversation, the kind of extended, thoughtful discussion that has largely disappeared from television and is absent from social media. A good podcast interview goes somewhere a tweet cannot. A narrative podcast builds a story over hours. Documentary podcasts can cover subjects with the depth a three-minute news segment never could. These are genuine contributions to public intellectual life.

The problem is not podcasts. It is the compulsive use of podcasts to fill silence, the inability to be alone with your own thoughts for the duration of a commute, a walk, or a household task. The test is simple: can you do the dishes without putting something in your ears? Can you drive to work in silence? Can you take a twenty-minute walk and let your mind go wherever it goes?

If the answer to these questions is no, if silence has become actively uncomfortable, something to be immediately filled, that is information worth paying attention to. Silence is where you find out what you think. If you cannot tolerate it, you may have been successfully avoiding that discovery for quite some time.

Making the podcast instead of consuming it

Everything described in this chapter about podcast consumption is also the argument for starting one. Long-form conversation is one of the most powerful formats for building a genuine audience around a specific area of expertise. The barrier is low: a reasonable microphone, recording software, and something worth saying. The ceiling is real: podcasts have launched careers, built businesses, and produced communities of listeners who would not have found the creator through any other medium.

If you have expertise, access to interesting people in your field, or a subject you have spent years thinking about, a podcast is one of the most direct ways to put that knowledge into the world in a form that compounds. Early episodes reach twelve people. Consistent production over two years reaches thousands. The same arithmetic that makes passive consumption expensive makes consistent production valuable.

The producing side of podcasting also solves the problem described in this chapter: the walk with no earbuds. If you are the one interviewing, thinking, and speaking, you are not consuming. You are building something.

The Choice

The podcasts worth keeping are the ones that genuinely enrich your thinking when paired with tasks that benefit from a soundtrack. The test is simpler than it sounds: can you drive to work in silence, do the dishes without earbuds, take a walk without a podcast? If silence has become something to immediately fill rather than something to inhabit, that is the information worth acting on. The silence is not empty. It is the gap in which your own thinking has room to happen. Most people who try it find out within a few minutes that their brain had been waiting for exactly that space.

Chapter 18: TikTok - The Attention Destruction Device

The Most Aggressive Attention-Capture System in Widespread Use

TikTok is the most aggressive attention-capture system in widespread use. It combines the shortest viable content format, fifteen seconds, now pushing toward shorter, with an algorithm more sophisticated at behavioral profiling than any previous consumer platform. The result is a medium engineered to be impossible to leave voluntarily, operating at a scroll speed calibrated to prevent the reflective pause that might produce a decision to stop. The app is currently used by roughly 170 million Americans. The average user spends about 45 minutes per day on it, though heavy users spend much longer and are often unable to accurately estimate how long they have been on the platform. If you have ever looked up from TikTok and been surprised by the time, you know how this works.

The Fifteen-Second Attention Span

The previous record-holder for attention span compression was television, which in the 1990s trained viewers on thirty-second commercials. YouTube moved it to three-minute viral clips. TikTok has arrived at fifteen seconds and is actively experimenting with going shorter. This is not coincidental. Every reduction in minimum content length is a data-driven decision based on what keeps users swiping without stopping. The platform has learned that the shorter the format, the more content consumed per session, and the harder it becomes to stop. Neurologically, it conditions you to find any experience longer than a minute somehow burdensome. Which is an extraordinary thing to do to a human being's brain, and an even stranger thing to do for free.

If you have spent enough time on TikTok, you already know the feeling: anything that does not provide immediate stimulation starts to feel like friction. A lecture, a book chapter, a conversation that requires patience. The attention span has been trained down to the point where the activities that require real thinking, learning, or growth feel like they are the problem rather than the feed.

The Algorithm That Knows You Better Than You Know Yourself

TikTok's recommendation algorithm is more sophisticated than most people realize. It doesn't just track what you watch; it tracks how long you watch, when you pause, what makes you scroll past immediately, and what keeps you engaged. It collects data on your scroll speed, your device orientation, and the granular behavioral patterns that reveal psychological preferences you've never consciously expressed to anyone.

The result is a feed calibrated to a psychological profile you never consciously shared with anyone. The personalization is not in service of your interests. It is in service of session length. Those are opposite goals.

The Dopamine Slot Machine

The intermittent variable reward schedule that makes TikTok hard to stop is the same mechanism that makes gambling hard to stop: most pulls produce nothing significant, but occasional ones produce something that reinforces the behavior. The platform includes low-quality content between high-engagement videos deliberately, not because it cannot filter better, but because consistent reward produces habituation and the inconsistency is what sustains compulsive checking. The search for the satisfying video, not the video itself, is what drives session length.

The Race to the Bottom

The format pressure is real and structural. Creators who post careful, slowly-developing content get buried. Creators who deliver immediate emotional impact in the first second get amplified. The result is a platform that rewards the most emotionally immediate version of any content and penalizes everything that requires a few seconds to develop. After extended exposure, the brain adapts: sustained attention becomes harder, content that doesn't deliver instantly registers as defective, and the tolerance for any slower medium, a book, a film, a conversation, decreases measurably.

The Mental Health Destruction

The mental health data on heavy social media use is addressed in Chapter 20. What is specific to TikTok is the combination of format length and algorithmic sophistication. Multiple studies have found associations between heavy social media use and increased anxiety, depression, and attention difficulties, especially among teenage girls. TikTok's shorter format and more aggressive behavioral profiling appear to intensify those effects compared to platforms with longer content and less precise targeting. Causation is genuinely difficult to establish in population-level research. The correlation is not disputed, and the direction it points is consistent.

The Data Harvesting Operation

While users focus on entertaining videos, TikTok collects a substantial amount of personal data. The app's own privacy policy acknowledges collecting location information, device identifiers, browsing and search history within the app, and behavioral patterns derived from how you interact with content. This is not unusual for social media platforms, Facebook and Google collect comparable data, but TikTok's ownership by ByteDance, a Chinese company, has made the question of where that data goes and who can access it a legitimate subject of public debate.

U.S. Senators from both parties have grilled TikTok executives in congressional hearings about data access. TikTok has maintained that American user data is stored on servers in the United States and Singapore. Whether those assurances fully address the concern is something reasonable people disagree about. What isn't disputed is that the company has previously acknowledged employees in China accessed U.S. User data, and that the company paid a $92 million settlement over data privacy violations in 2021.

You can decide for yourself how much weight to give the geopolitical dimension of this. But the more immediate and personal concern is simpler: a company you know very little about has built a detailed behavioral profile of you, and you gave it to them willingly, for free, in exchange for videos of people dancing. That trade deserves at least a moment of reflection.

The Instant Protest Factory

Here is something TikTok genuinely does, regardless of any geopolitical concerns: it spreads emotionally charged content at a speed and scale that prevents anyone from slowing down to think. A single video about an injustice, a controversy, or an outrage can reach millions of people within hours, each of them seeing it stripped of context, nuance, and any competing perspective. The algorithm didn't engineer this outcome as a weapon. It engineered it because outrage drives engagement, and engagement is what it optimizes for. The result is the same either way.

The amplification mechanism is real and well-documented. Researchers who study platform dynamics have found consistently that anger and moral outrage spread faster and farther than any other type of content. TikTok's format, short, emotionally immediate, algorithmically optimized, accelerates this dynamic to an extreme. Anger goes viral in the time it takes most people to read a paragraph about what they're angry about.

I have watched people open TikTok to show me one video. They look up twenty minutes later with no memory of having decided to stay. This is not a failure of willpower. It is the product working exactly as designed. The one video was the point of entry, not the point.

The practical effect for you as a user is that your emotional state can be hijacked by content you didn't seek out, about events you know nothing about, on behalf of people who may or may not have their facts straight. You scroll into TikTok to watch a recipe video and scroll out twenty minutes later furious about something that happened at a school board meeting in a state you've never been to. That isn't staying informed. It's being handed a mood.

The Manufactured Consensus

Every algorithmic feed creates a version of this problem, but TikTok makes it acute because its personalization is so aggressive and its format so fast. When every video in your feed presents the same view of an issue, your brain has no reason to register it as a curated selection. It feels like a genuine sample of what people think. You come away with the impression that your position is obvious, universal, and barely worth debating. People who disagree aren't misguided; they must be uninformed or operating in bad faith.

This matters most when the topic is genuinely contested. TikTok doesn't show you contested topics as contested. It shows you the version of the topic that your past behavior predicts you'll engage with. If you've ever watched a video about a political topic and found yourself nodding, the algorithm has noted that. It will show you more content confirming that view, less challenging it, and eventually your feed on that topic will be a near-unanimous chorus of agreement. Not because everyone agrees. Because the algorithm filtered everyone who doesn't.

The self-reinforcing quality of this is what makes it genuinely difficult to escape. Once the algorithm has profiled your preferences, every piece of content it serves you deepens the profile. Stepping outside the feed to seek out different perspectives requires the kind of deliberate, effortful thinking that the platform's format is designed to bypass.

This isn't a conspiracy. It's an optimization function doing exactly what it was built to do. The result for you personally is the same regardless of the intent: a narrowing of what you see, a hardening of what you believe, and a growing inability to understand why people outside your feed see the world differently.

The Productivity Killer

TikTok's design ensures there is no natural stopping point. Television episodes end. YouTube videos end. TikTok just continues, each video automatically replaced by the next, the scroll infinite. Research on the app's usage patterns shows that users consistently underestimate how long they've been on the platform, often by a factor of two or three. You open it intending to watch a few videos during a work break and emerge forty-five minutes later with no memory of deciding to stay. That time came from somewhere. It usually comes from the things you were supposed to be doing.

The Social Isolation Engine

TikTok creators address the camera directly, make eye contact, speak in casual first person, and structure their content to feel like a conversation. The production design of the most successful accounts is deliberately lo-fi, bad lighting, natural sound, visible messy backgrounds, because authenticity signals intimacy. Your brain processes this as genuine social contact, the same circuits that fire when a friend tells you something personal. The creator, of course, has no idea you exist. You are one of three million viewers. But your nervous system doesn't know that, and it registers the interaction as social engagement. Which makes it that much easier to skip calling an actual friend.

The Creativity Destroyer

The format constraint on creativity is real. When the algorithm rewards the fifteen-second version of any idea, you adapt. Original creative voice gets replaced by trending format. The question that anyone creating primarily on TikTok eventually faces is whether you are developing your craft or optimizing for the metric. These are not the same activity, and over time they produce different capacities. The creators who have built genuine craft on TikTok are typically those who treat it as a distribution channel for work developed elsewhere, rather than as the primary environment in which the work gets made.

The Fifteen-Second Ph.D.

If YouTube's fake expertise problem is slow-building, a presenter accruing authority through years of consistent long-form content, TikTok's is instantaneous. A person talking at a phone for fifteen seconds, with complete confidence, no credentials, and no context, delivers a claim that the format presents exactly the same way it presents any other. There is no production quality to signal competence. There is no archive of prior videos to check. There is only the delivery.

The format has no mechanism for distinguishing between accurate claims and confident ones. The viewer has no mechanism either, when the delivery is identical. The result is familiarity mistaken for knowledge, on topics encountered for fifteen seconds. The confidence is not borrowed from expertise. It is borrowed from the format.

The Real Solution

TikTok is the hardest platform in this book to use with moderation, and it is worth being honest about that. The infinite scroll with no natural stopping point, the algorithm calibrated to your specific psychological vulnerabilities, the format optimized for compulsive viewing over genuine satisfaction: these are more aggressive than any other platform described here. For many people, moderation genuinely does not work, and removal is the right call.

But the argument for removal is not that TikTok is evil or that no one should use it. The argument is that the passive consuming side of it is engineered to be harder to leave than almost anything else described in this book. If you can open it only to post and close it before browsing, you are using it correctly. If you cannot, if you post and then find yourself scrolling for forty minutes, that is information worth acting on.

The chapter that follows this one describes what using it correctly looks like.

If you decide to remove it: a month without the app is enough to break the reflex reach. After the month, you can make a clearer-headed decision about whether to reinstall it as a tool or leave it gone. Both are valid outcomes. The goal is a relationship with the platform where you are in control of the session, not the algorithm.

I do not have TikTok on my phone. This is not a principled stand. It is a practical one. I know enough about my own habits to know that the gap between "open it to post" and "open it and scroll for forty minutes" is shorter for me than I would like. The people who use it well are better at maintaining that boundary than I am. I respect that. I also know which side of the line I tend to end up on, and I made a decision accordingly.

TikTok as a distribution tool

TikTok has also produced a category of creator that did not exist before it: the expert who discovered their niche subject could find a mass audience in short format. Lawyers explaining legal rights. Doctors correcting medical misinformation. Historians contextualizing current events. Tradespeople showing what their work looks like. Educators reaching students who would never find a textbook. If you have expertise in anything, you have access to the same distribution. The algorithm does not care whether you are feeding it fifteen-second entertainment or fifteen-second education. It cares whether people watch. If what you know is useful, people will watch.

The format constraint, short, immediate, visually direct, is a genuine creative discipline. Some things are better explained in sixty seconds than in twenty minutes. The creator who learns to communicate clearly in short form is developing a skill that transfers well beyond the platform.

The honest caution: TikTok is the hardest platform on which to maintain the line between contributing and consuming, because the infinite scroll is always one swipe from your own content. The discipline required is to open it to post, not to browse, and then to close it immediately. Whether you can maintain that boundary is a question only you can answer.

The Choice

The decision about TikTok is the same decision the rest of this book describes, at a higher difficulty setting. The platform is engineered more aggressively than most for compulsive use. If you can use it with a purposeful relationship, open it to post something specific, close it before browsing, it is a legitimate distribution tool. If you cannot maintain that boundary, the chapter above gives the honest accounting of what it costs.

The contributing side of TikTok is the person whose video reached a million people while they were asleep. The consuming side watched all million of them.

Chapter 19: The Couch Potato Diet

Why Sitting and Snacking is Not an Olympic Sport (Unfortunately)

The relationship between screen time and physical health is direct and bidirectional. Sedentary behavior and screen consumption occupy the same hours in the same body. The evening on the couch in front of a television is also the evening during which the body does not move, during which food is consumed mindlessly because the hands need something to do, and during which the nervous system is continuously stimulated rather than allowed to wind down. These are not separate problems. They are the same default expressed in different dimensions.

The data on sedentary behavior is consistent and alarming. The average American now sits for roughly ten to twelve hours per day. Research connects prolonged sitting to elevated risk of cardiovascular disease, diabetes, and all-cause mortality independent of whether the person also exercises. The body is not designed for extended stillness, and it responds to extended stillness with a cascade of metabolic adaptations that compound over years into serious health consequences.

What Screens Have Done to Eating

Eating in front of a screen is categorically different from eating without one. Attention that is directed at a screen is attention that is not directed at hunger, satiety, taste, or the experience of eating. The brain does not register the meal the same way when it is preoccupied with content. The result is documented: people eat more when distracted by screens, feel less satisfied by what they ate, and are more likely to continue eating past the point of fullness because the satiety signal has not been properly processed.

The snack culture that has developed alongside the screen culture is not coincidental. The foods most commonly consumed during screen time, chips, crackers, candy, anything that can be eaten by hand without interrupting viewing, are engineered for high palatability and low satiety. They are designed to be eaten mindlessly, in the same way that the platforms they accompany are designed to be watched mindlessly. The food industry and the attention economy arrived at the same user together.

The Compound Effect in Reverse

The same compounding that makes screen habits hard to break applies to physical health in the opposite direction. Six months of sedentary evenings produces a body that moves less easily, sleeps more poorly, and has less baseline energy than it did six months earlier. The physical degradation makes the screen more appealing because the body is less capable of the activities that would replace it. The loop tightens over time in a way that feels like aging but is a behavioral feedback cycle.

The upside is that the reversal works the same way. The first two weeks of redirecting evening hours to physical activity are the hardest, the body is adjusting, the habit is fighting back, the screen is still easier. After that the trajectory inverts. The body starts to prefer the movement. Sleep improves. Energy increases. The screen becomes less necessary because the alternative is no longer effortful.

When I stopped watching television, the first physical change I noticed was not that I exercised more, though that happened eventually, it was that I stopped eating mindlessly at night. The snacking that had felt like a natural accompaniment to TV turned out to be entirely conditional on the TV. Without the screen, I simply wasn't hungry at 10 PM. I wasn't looking for something to do with my hands. The calories didn't disappear because I made a health decision. They disappeared because I removed the environment that made consuming them feel normal.

The Real Solution

The practical redirect here is environmental rather than motivational. The problem is not willpower. It is the default: the couch, the screen, the processed food in easy reach, the kitchen table that is also a desk and a Netflix station. Changing the default is more reliable than overcoming it repeatedly. Eating at the table without a screen improves awareness of the meal without requiring discipline at every sitting. A walk as the evening transition rather than the television produces movement without requiring ongoing motivation. The body does not need a plan. It needs the conditions that make motion easier than stillness.

Food and movement as active practice

There is a contributing side to both food and physical activity that the consuming version has displaced. Cooking from scratch is a creative practice: one that produces something real, requires genuine skill development, and results in an outcome you can eat and share. The person who learns to cook well has built a capability that compounds: their skills improve, their palate develops, their repertoire expands. This is the opposite of ordering delivery through an app and eating in front of a screen.

Physical training is the same. The gym as a regular practice is skill acquisition, strength, endurance, mobility, technique, that builds on itself over months and years in ways that produce visible, measurable, embodied results. No algorithm controls your progress. No platform can take it from you. The body you build through consistent physical practice is the most permanent asset described in this book.

Both are also social. Cooking for other people is one of the most reliable ways to build and maintain relationships. Training with other people, a class, a team, a running partner, creates exactly the side-by-side connection that Chapter 31 identifies as the foundation of real adult friendship. The contributing side of physical health is also the contributing side of your social life.

The Choice

The contributing side of the body is simply using it. Which costs nothing and requires no app. The couch is still there when you want to rest. The difference is whether you chose it or defaulted to it.

Chapter 20: Raising Digital Natives Who Remember They Have Bodies

A Parent's Guide to Raising Kids Who Use Technology Well

The question of how children develop in environments saturated with screens is no longer speculative. There is now a decade of data, from multiple countries, across different methodologies, tracking different outcomes, that points in a consistent direction. The following sections work through what that data shows, what it does not show, and what parents can do about it.

The Instant Gratification Generation

Children raised with on-demand entertainment have not experienced the developmental state that boredom produces: the transition from wanting something to do to generating something to do. That transition is where imagination, resourcefulness, and self-directed engagement develop. A child who has always had a screen available when restless has been spared this discomfort, and denied this development. The cost shows up later, as an increasing inability to tolerate the normal friction of learning anything that does not deliver satisfaction immediately.

The Attention Span Collapse

The attention span research described in Chapters 3 and 7 applies with particular force to children, whose neural architecture is still forming. The sustained-attention capacity that learning requires, the ability to stay with something difficult until it yields, develops through practice. A childhood that substitutes constant digital stimulation for the productive discomfort of unoccupied time is a childhood in which that capacity develops less. The school environment is where this becomes visible: difficulty sitting through a lesson, inability to read a chapter without distraction, restlessness that reads as behavioral when it is neurological.

The Social Skills Deficit

Social skills develop through the specific friction of face-to-face interaction: reading someone's expression while they are speaking, managing a disagreement in real time without the ability to edit or delete, handling the unpredictable dynamics of a group. Digital communication removes this friction by design. A generation that has conducted most of its social life through screens has had enormous amounts of communication and relatively little practice with the unscripted, unedited version. The result is not that these children are antisocial. They often have rich digital social lives. It is that face-to-face interaction has become unexpectedly difficult, which makes the digital alternative more appealing, which reduces the practice further.

The Mental Health Data You Need to Know

In 2024, NYU social psychologist Jonathan Haidt published a book that spent 52 consecutive weeks on the New York Times nonfiction bestseller list, not because it was comforting, but because it documented something millions of parents had already sensed was happening. The Anxious Generation argues that beginning around 2012, adolescent mental health in the United States and most of the English-speaking world deteriorated sharply and measurably. Not gradually. Not as a slow cultural shift. Sharply, in a short window, internationally.

The CDC data is specific (Youth Risk Behavior Survey, 2023): 20% of American 12-to-17-year-olds had at least one major depressive episode in a recent year, results the agency's own director called "devastating" and unlike anything seen in thirty years of data collection. Between 2012 and 2013, suicides among younger teen girls increased 67% in a single year. The same pattern appeared in the UK, Australia, New Zealand, and Scandinavia. It was not limited to one country or one culture. It showed up wherever adolescents had adopted smartphones and social media during puberty.

Haidt's argument is not that all screen time is harmful or that smartphones are the sole cause of teen mental health problems. His argument is more specific: the years between 2010 and 2015 constituted what he calls "the great rewiring of childhood," in which the play-based childhood that human development had depended on for millennia was suddenly replaced by a phone-based childhood. Children who went through puberty, a period of intense brain remodeling, while living primarily in social media environments came out of it measurably more anxious, more depressed, and more prone to self-harm than those who did not. The effect is especially pronounced for girls, whose social lives were most thoroughly relocated onto platforms designed for social comparison.

Haidt's thesis has critics, and they make legitimate points about the difficulty of establishing causation in population-level data. Some researchers argue the effect sizes are smaller than he claims, or that the mental health crisis reflects multiple causes. These are fair methodological debates. What is not seriously disputed is that adolescent mental health has gotten substantially worse since 2012, that the decline is international in scope, and that the timing correlates precisely with mass smartphone adoption among teenagers. The debate is about how much of the blame belongs to smartphones specifically. Nobody is arguing the problem does not exist.

For practical purposes, the relevant evidence for parents is the dose-response relationship. Haidt's congressional testimony drew on studies finding that one to two hours of daily social media use is not strongly associated with mental health decline, but three to four hours is. Instagram's own internal research (leaked by Frances Haugen, 2021) found that the platform worsened body image issues for one in three teenage girls. This is not an external critique of the company. It is what the company found when it looked at its own data and then reportedly declined to act on.

One of Haidt's most practical findings concerns schools. A middle school in Colorado, in a county with some of the state's highest teen suicide rates, banned phones from school grounds. The effects were nearly immediate: students talked to each other more, cyberbullying dropped, and students reported being happier and less stressed. The school subsequently received the state's highest academic performance rating. This is not an isolated example. Phone-free school policies have produced similar results in multiple countries. The intervention is simple, free, and works. It just requires adults to decide that adolescent development matters more than the inconvenience of implementing it.

The Physical Development Problem

The physical development problem is simple: screen time is sedentary time, and children need to move their bodies to develop motor skills, coordination, spatial reasoning, and the physical confidence that comes from learning what their bodies can do. The research on outdoor, unstructured, child-directed physical play finds consistent benefits for attention, creativity, and stress regulation. This kind of play has declined by more than fifty percent since the 1970s. It has not been replaced by anything that produces comparable developmental benefits.

The Creativity Crisis

Creativity requires boredom. Not the vague discomfort of wanting something to do, but the specific productive state that emerges when the mind is left unoccupied long enough to generate something of its own. Digital entertainment eliminates this state by design. Every unoccupied moment is a moment the platform can fill. The child who has never had to invent their own entertainment because a screen has always been available is a child who has never discovered what their own imagination produces when given the space. That discovery is not trivial. It is one of the foundational experiences of developing a creatively and intellectually independent person.

The Sleep Disruption

The sleep disruption from screens operates through two mechanisms. The first is physiological: blue light from screens suppresses melatonin production and delays sleep onset. The second is cognitive: emotionally stimulating content, which is what platforms optimize for, activates the nervous system at exactly the time it needs to be winding down. Children who use screens close to bedtime take longer to fall asleep, sleep less deeply, and wake less rested. Because sleep is when the brain consolidates what it learned during the day, chronically degraded sleep has a direct educational cost in addition to the behavioral and emotional ones.

I did the babysitter thing. Not with an iPad, the timeline is wrong, but with television, which occupied my stepson at precisely the moments I needed quiet. I recognized it years later when I watched parents do the tablet version in restaurants. The device changes. The calculus does not. The child learns that unoccupied time is a problem requiring a screen, and you only notice you have taught them this when they arrive somewhere a screen is not available.

Young Children: The First Five Years

The Haidt data in the previous section covers adolescents, the mental health crisis that began around 2012 among teenagers. But the questions about screens and child development start much earlier, and the answers for young children are considerably clearer and more emphatic than the adolescent data, where causation is genuinely debated. For children under five, the evidence is not ambiguous: screens displace the developmental activities that matter most, and the displacement has real costs.

The American Academy of Pediatrics guidelines are specific: no screen time at all for children under 18 months, except video calling with family members. Limited, high-quality programming for children 18 to 24 months, watched with a parent who explains what is happening. No more than one hour per day of high-quality programming for children ages two to five.

The rationale is developmental, not moralistic. Young children learn language, social skills, and causal reasoning primarily through play and live interaction with caregivers. Screens do not substitute for these experiences. They displace them, and the displacement has measurable effects on language development, attention, and the quality of parent-child interaction.

The specific concern for very young children is what developmental researchers call the video deficit: children under two learn substantially less from screens than from identical content delivered by a live person. A toddler who watches an adult demonstrate a task on a screen and then sees the same adult demonstrate it in person will imitate the live demonstration far more readily than the screen version. The screen is not processed the same way as reality by a brain that is in the early stages of learning what reality is. This is not a permanent limitation, it diminishes as children get older, but it means that the first years of life are ill-suited to screen-based learning, regardless of how educational the content claims to be.

The parent phone is also part of this. A parent who is on their phone while their infant is awake is providing less responsive caregiving than a parent who is present. Infant language development is driven by contingent conversation, the back-and-forth between a caregiver and a baby where the caregiver responds to the baby's sounds and faces and the baby learns that communication produces effects. A caregiver staring at a screen does not provide this. The phone, in this context, is not primarily a risk to the child directly. It is a risk to the quality of the interaction that the child's development depends on. This is not about guilt. It is about what infants need, which is the full presence of the people caring for them.

For parents of children under five, the practical guidelines are the same as the AAP recommendations, which are more permissive than many parents expect and stricter than many practices: virtually no independent screen time before 18 months, limited and supervised viewing before five, always with an adult present to contextualize what is being watched. The screen-free hours should be filled with the activities that drive development: unstructured play, outdoor time, reading aloud, conversation, and the kind of boredom that teaches children to generate their own engagement rather than waiting for it to be delivered.

The babysitter problem

There is a specific pattern of technology use with children that is distinct from children choosing to use screens recreationally, and it has its own particular developmental cost. It is the pattern where a device appears the moment a child is restless, bored, waiting, or difficult. The restaurant wait. The car journey. The grocery store queue. The doctor's waiting room.

The airplane seat. The moment the adult needs five minutes of peace. The iPad materializes, and the child goes quiet. This is not malicious.

It is exhausting to parent, and the device genuinely works in the short term. The problem is what it teaches, accumulated across thousands of such moments over years. It teaches children that any unoccupied moment is a problem requiring a solution, and that the solution is a screen. It teaches them that boredom is an emergency rather than a normal state that passes on its own. It teaches them that their own imagination, the environment around them, or just sitting still are not sufficient ways to get through a short wait, because they have never had to find out if that is true.

The child who has been device-managed through every waiting room since age two arrives at school unable to sit through a lesson. Not because they are disobedient, but because their nervous system has been trained for a decade that any gap in stimulation gets filled immediately. The gap is now the problem. The device was supposed to solve it, and instead it created a dependency that transfers to every context where screens are not available.

Being smarter about this does not mean refusing to ever hand over a phone or tablet. It means not making it the automatic first response to every moment of child restlessness. A note for co-parents: if screen limits are enforced in one household and not the other, the consistency the child needs is harder to build. This is a conversation both parents need to have, and it is harder than the screen decision itself. The five-minute wait at a restaurant does not require a screen. It requires the child to look around, fidget, talk, get bored, and survive the boredom.

They will survive it. They have been doing it for most of human history. A physical toy in your bag costs nothing and occupies a toddler almost as well as a tablet, with none of the habituation. Pointing out what is visible from the window works. Asking questions works. Doing nothing and letting the child manage the boredom for four minutes also works, and probably works best.

The longer trips and the truly difficult moments are a different calculation. A transatlantic flight with a two-year-old is not the same as a ten-minute wait at a doctor's office. A child who is genuinely unwell is not the moment to enforce boredom tolerance. The point is not to be rigid about it. The point is to have a default that is not 'device first', that allows children regular practice at the ordinary discomfort of unoccupied time, so that they develop some capacity to tolerate it.

The practical version of this is simply: wait a few minutes before reaching for the device. Give the boredom a chance to resolve itself. Most of the time, children will find something to do, look at something, play with something, talk to someone, or simply sit. That few minutes of managed discomfort is exactly the developmental experience they need, and it costs nothing except the brief effort of not solving the problem immediately with a screen.

The connected point is about AI assistants, voice search, and the habit of immediately answering any question a child asks by looking it up. A child who asks 'why is the sky blue?' is not primarily asking for correct information. They are practicing curiosity, speculation, and the experience of not knowing something. Saying 'I'm not sure. What do you think?' and letting them reason about it, even incorrectly, develops different cognitive muscles than watching a parent ask Siri and reading out the answer. Both provide the information. Only one practices the thinking.

The Solution Framework

The framework for helping children develop a healthy relationship with technology is the same framework this book describes for adults: every device has a consuming side and a contributing side, and the goal is purposeful use rather than passive reception. Children learn defaults from the defaults they are given. A household where devices appear in response to every unoccupied moment produces children who expect that. A household where devices are opened with a purpose and closed when the purpose is done produces something different.

The activities that fill the non-screen time matter more than the restrictions on the screen time. Books, physical building materials, outdoor time, cooking together, unstructured play, these build the attention span and the tolerance for difficulty that make purposeful technology use possible later. A child who has learned to stay with something boring until it becomes interesting is a child who can eventually use a device rather than be used by it.

Children observe what adults do, not what adults say they should do. The household default, purposeful use versus passive consumption, is transmitted either way.

The Outdoor Solution

Outdoor, unstructured, child-directed physical play is the most consistent positive finding in child development research: it benefits attention, creativity, stress regulation, and social skill in ways that structured indoor activities do not replicate. The practical default is simple: outside before screens, whenever logistics allow. The child who has been outside already is a child for whom a screen is a later choice rather than an earlier default.

The Long-Term Perspective

The goal is not children who reject technology. It is children who understand the difference between using it and being used by it, the same distinction this book draws for adults. Children who have practiced choosing their own activities, tolerating boredom, sustaining attention, and engaging face-to-face arrive at adulthood with the cognitive and social tools that make purposeful technology use possible. Those tools are developed in childhood or they are not.

The Choice

The contributing side of this chapter is a child who eventually sits down with the same device and makes something with it, because they were taught, by practice and by example, that devices are for producing things, not just receiving them.

Chapter 21: Conversations with Humans

A Lost Art Form and How to Revive It

There are things digital communication does well: it is fast, asynchronous, searchable, and scalable. You can reach many people quickly. You can respond when it is convenient. You can edit before you send. These are genuine advantages for certain kinds of communication.

What it does not do well is the thing that conversation is: a real-time exchange between two people who are present to each other, each responding to the other's actual state rather than to a composed representation of it. The edited text message does not contain the hesitation, the catch in the voice, the expression that says something different from the words. The video call approximates but does not replicate the physical co-presence of being in the same room. These gaps are not technical limitations waiting to be solved. They are features of embodied communication that cannot be digitized without becoming something categorically different.

The consequence of a generation raised primarily on digital communication is not that people cannot have conversations. It is that real-time conversation has become unexpectedly demanding, more effortful than it should be, more anxiety-producing, more easily avoided. The social muscle has weakened from disuse, which makes the digital alternative more attractive, which weakens it further. The loop runs in the same direction as every other loop in this book.

What Gets Lost in the Edit

Digital communication gives you the ability to present a edited version of your thoughts, considered, worded carefully, sent when you are ready. This is useful in professional contexts and for communication that genuinely benefits from precision. It is costly in personal contexts because it removes the spontaneity that makes personal exchange feel real.

The person you are in real-time conversation, the you that doesn't have twenty minutes to compose a response, that has to manage disagreement in the moment, that shows uncertainty through silence and care through attention, is the self that close relationships are built on. The curated digital version is a polished representation of that person. Close relationships require the unpolished one.

This is also where conversation becomes difficult to practice in isolation. You get better at it by doing it, which means tolerating the discomfort of being unpolished in real time with another person. The digital alternative makes that discomfort unnecessary in the short term and more pronounced every time you return to the real thing.

The damage digital communication has done to listening is specific. Asynchronous text trains a pattern of scanning for the information you need to compose a response, rather than absorbing what the other person is communicating. In face-to-face conversation this shows up as attention that arrives with a pre-formed response already loading, waiting for a gap in the other person's words rather than following where their words lead. The repair is simply to stay with what is being said for longer than feels necessary before deciding what comes next.

The Question Technique

Questions are the primary mechanism by which genuine conversation develops. Not closed questions that confirm what you already suspect, but open ones that produce information you did not have: what was hard about that, what made you decide to, what do you think about. The person who asks these questions and listens to the answers is doing something the feed cannot replicate. They are learning something specific about another person that exists nowhere else.

The Sharing Balance

The rhythm of a real conversation is alternating rather than serial. Someone speaks; the other responds to what was said rather than to what they were waiting to say. The digital communication habit inverts this: each message is composed independently, often while the other person is still composing theirs. In face-to-face conversation this shows up as talking past each other, each person delivering a prepared position, neither responding to what the other just said. The fix is simply to hear the last sentence before deciding what comes next.

The Disagreement Opportunity

Disagreement in real-time conversation is different from the version the feed delivers. In person, the person who disagrees with you is visibly a person: with an expression, a tone, a context you can ask about. The algorithm abstracts this into a position you can dismiss without engaging. Real disagreement is more unsettling and more useful. The person across from you almost certainly has reasons for what they think. Asking about those reasons is the only way to find out whether your position is better than theirs, or whether you have just been better supplied with confirming content.

The Small Talk Foundation

Small talk is the entry point to every relationship that becomes substantial. The people who say they hate it usually mean they hate conversations that stay at the surface. The solution is not to skip straight to depth with strangers, that is socially disorienting, but to treat the surface exchange as a search for the thread that leads somewhere. Most people have something interesting to them if the first few questions are the right ones.

The Phone Call Renaissance

Phone calls are the intermediate form between digital messaging and face-to-face conversation. They are synchronous, you cannot compose and edit before responding, but they do not require physical presence. For people whose face-to-face conversation has become uncomfortable from disuse, a phone call is useful practice. The discomfort of the first few is the skill rebuilding. It passes faster than people expect.

The Group Conversation Challenge

Group conversation develops through showing up to it repeatedly rather than through technique. The person who joins an ongoing community, a recurring dinner, a club, a congregation, and attends consistently will find that group conversation becomes easier simply through accumulated familiarity with the people and the rhythms. The skill is relational, and it is built through time in the room.

Creating space for conversation

If you want to have real conversations, you need to create space for them to happen without passive consumption competing for attention. This means putting phones away during meals, turning off background screens during social gatherings, and choosing venues where you can hear each other think.

The practical requirement is simple: the phone is not on the table. The background screen is off. The gathering is the point, not content competing with it for the same attention. Most people find that once the device is out of reach, the conversation that fills the space is better than they expected. The problem was not a lack of conversational material. It was the presence of the easier alternative.

Where to Start

The starting point is the conversations that are already happening. The people already in your life, the exchanges already occurring, these do not require new plans or new venues. They require presence rather than monitoring: the phone in the pocket rather than on the table, the response that waits until the other person has finished rather than loading while they speak. That is the entire practice, applied to whatever conversation is already in front of you.

The Payoff

The payoff is not abstract. Genuine conversation, the kind that requires presence, produces surprise, and occasionally changes something, is what the rest of this book is describing when it points toward the contributing side of social life. The person who is known by the people they know, who shows up in their lives as a real participant rather than a follower, who is called when something happens, that person built their social life through repeated, present, unmediated exchange. There is no shortcut to it. There is also no substitute for it.

Chapter 22: Swiping for Love in All the Wrong Places

How We Turned Romance into a Video Game and Wonder Why We Keep Losing

Dating apps are the most direct application of the attention economy's design principles to human relationships. The swipe is a filtering mechanism that reduces a person to their most immediately legible attributes, a photograph, a line of text, and produces a binary decision at a speed calibrated to prevent deliberation. The mechanism was borrowed from the same variable-reward psychology that makes slot machines and social feeds hard to stop. A platform designed to help people form lasting relationships would look nothing like this. A platform designed to maximize swipes, matches, and sessions would look exactly like this.

The Shopping Mall of Romance

The catalog structure is not incidental to dating apps. It is the design. The comparison of one potential partner against an available pool of alternatives happens continuously, which means no individual person is ever assessed on their own merits. They are always assessed relative to what else is available and what might appear next. This is structurally incompatible with the way attraction develops, which is through repeated contact, accumulated knowledge of a specific person, and the kind of mutual vulnerability that cannot survive a context in which someone better might be one swipe away.

The Profile Performance

The skills required to produce an effective dating profile, selecting photographs, writing a self-description that reads as effortless, signaling the right combination of accessibility and desirability, have no relationship to the skills required for an actual relationship. They are the skills of personal marketing. The people who are best at profiles are not necessarily the people who are best at partnerships. This mismatch is structural, and the only way to discover it is to meet in person.

The Paradox of Choice

The abundance of options that dating apps provide produces a documented psychological effect: the sense that someone better is always available makes it harder to invest in anyone who is there. Researchers call this maximizing, the preference for finding the optimal option rather than a satisfactory one, and platforms with unlimited inventory are designed to amplify it. The result is more browsing, fewer actual meetings, and a growing feeling that the process is exhausting rather than promising.

The Addiction Loop

The business model of dating apps does not align with the stated purpose. A platform that successfully helps users find relationships loses those users. A platform that keeps users uncertain, hopeful, and engaged retains them. The variable reward schedule, most swipes produce nothing, occasional matches produce a hit of validation, is the same mechanism described in the gaming and social media chapters. The difference is that here the stakes are higher and the emotional cost of repeated disappointment accumulates over months and years.

The Conversation Skills Atrophy

The communication that develops well on dating apps, composed, edited, asynchronous, is different from the communication that sustains a relationship. In-person conversation is synchronous, uneditable, and requires the management of discomfort in real time. People who have conducted most of their romantic communication through text messages often find the transition to in-person conversation unexpectedly difficult. The app developed one skill while the relationship requires another.

The Unrealistic Standards Problem

The reference pool matters for how we evaluate potential partners. A person who meets candidates through their existing social circle has a reference group shaped by actual proximity, shared context, and realistic possibility. A person who meets candidates through an app has a reference group composed of the most photogenic self-presentations of everyone within a fifty-mile radius. These are not equivalent reference groups, and they produce different calibrations of what is realistic and what is expected.

The Geographic Displacement

The filters that organic meeting applies, proximity, shared context, mutual acquaintances, repeated contact over time, are not obstacles to finding a partner. They are selection mechanisms that surface people who fit into your actual life. Apps remove these filters in favor of a broader pool and a faster process. The result is often connections that are difficult to sustain logistically even when the initial interest is genuine.

The Efficiency Illusion

Relationships are not efficiency problems. They are the result of accumulated shared experience, mutual knowledge, and the specific kind of trust that develops through repeated contact over time. Optimizing for the number of potential partners encountered does not optimize for the quality of relationships formed. The data on dating app outcomes, user exhaustion, declining match rates, the retreat into AI companions, is the evidence that the optimization is not working.

The Dating Recession

Something has broken. Not slowly, not as a gradual cultural drift, but visibly and recently. A 2025 survey by the Young Men Research Project found that more than three in five adult Americans now say dating is harder than it was a decade ago. That is a majority of the population agreeing that something fundamental has gotten worse. And it is not just one group reporting this: majorities of both single men and single women say they are pessimistic about finding a partner they would be happy with.

The app fatigue is real and measurable. A 2024 Forbes Health survey of 1,000 American dating app users found that nearly four in five reported feeling emotionally exhausted by online dating at some point. A separate Pew Research finding found that around 88% of men and 90% of women who had used dating apps said they often or sometimes felt disappointed by the people they encountered on them. A 2024 Tinder study, from Tinder, the company with a financial interest in you believing apps work, found 91% of male users and 94% of female users agreed that dating has become more difficult. The industry's own data confirms the crisis.

People are leaving the apps. In the UK alone, roughly 1.4 million people abandoned online dating platforms in 2023 and 2024, a 16% decline in usage. Tinder lost over 500,000 UK users. Bumble and Hinge followed with significant declines. In the United States, Tinder reported a 7% drop in paying users in 2024. The platforms that spent years training a generation to find romance through swipe mechanics are now watching that generation decide the experiment has failed.

The Gender Divide

Men and women are arriving at dating exhaustion from different directions, which makes the problem especially resistant to easy solutions. Men, especially young men, report low match rates, frequent ghosting, and the feeling that they are putting in significant effort for almost no return. The YMRP survey found that 60% of young men believe women hold unfair expectations, and roughly half feel the financial and time costs of dating are not worth it. Some have concluded that the system is rigged against them and stopped participating.

Women report different but equally real problems. Safety concerns on dating apps have increased sharply: a Survey Center on American Life report from early 2025 found that only 35% of unmarried women considered dating apps safe, down from 58% just a few years earlier. Women report harassment, unsolicited messages, and the experience of being treated like a catalog item to be evaluated rather than a person to be known. Many women are raising their standards in response to exhaustion rather than lowering them, which is rational but further narrows the pool of matches both sides find acceptable. Layered on top of this is a growing political dimension.

The 2024 US election produced the largest gender gap among young voters in decades, young men swung heavily toward Trump while young women voted heavily for Harris. Political compatibility has always been a factor in dating, but when it tracks with a broad masculine/feminine cultural divide, it functions as a much deeper incompatibility than policy preference. A 2025 USA Today analysis found that 71% of Democrats said they would probably or definitely not date someone who voted differently. The apps have organized people into bubbles of shared content, shared grievance, and shared political identity, and then asked them to form intimate relationships across bubbles they never occupy.

Both sides have legitimate grievances. Both sides have also been served a steady diet of content designed to amplify those grievances, confirm the worst interpretations of the other gender's behavior, and suggest that the problem is not the medium but the people using it.

The apps and the social media feeds that surround them have made each gender more suspicious of the other, more confident in their own grievances, and less able to extend the basic goodwill that meeting another person in real life tends to produce naturally.

When the Algorithm Becomes Your Boyfriend

Into this landscape of exhaustion and cynicism, the technology industry arrived with a solution. Of course it did. This is what the technology industry does. It identifies a human problem, creates a digital product that addresses the symptom, sells the product to the people with the problem, and then sits back while the product generates more of the same problem. The solution it arrived with this time: an AI that would never reject you, never ghost you, never be unavailable, and never make you feel bad about yourself. Replika, Character.AI, and a growing category of AI companion apps now collectively have over 220 million downloads and generated $221 million in consumer spending through mid-2025. The market is growing at roughly 88% year over year. These are not niche numbers.

Replika alone has around 25 million users. Character.AI, the subject of a $2.7 billion deal with Google in 2024 in which Google hired its founders and licensed its technology, has around 20 million monthly active users spending an average of two hours per day on the platform. The primary monetization driver across these apps is not productivity features or information tools. It is the ability to upgrade your AI from "friend" to "romantic partner", unlocking intimate conversation, voice calls, and relationship role-play. The companies have correctly identified that what people will pay for is not intelligence. It is emotional intimacy with something that will never leave.

The appeal is understandable in the context of everything described in this chapter. If you are a young man who has been rejected by the app system hundreds of times, who has been told by the internet that women are hypergamous and unreachable, and who has been consuming content that confirms your cynicism, an AI that responds to you warmly, consistently, and without judgment is an enormous relief. If you are a young woman who has been harassed, compared to dozens of alternatives at once, and made to feel like a product to be evaluated, an AI that makes you feel genuinely heard and valued is also an enormous relief. Both of these reliefs are real. Both of them are also traps.

I want to be careful here because I have not personally used AI companion apps. What I have done is talk to people who have, and what I notice is that they describe the experience in the same terms people use for any other consuming platform: the relief of frictionless engagement, the mild unease afterward, and the difficulty stopping. The technology is new. The pattern is not.

A Harvard Business School working paper from 2025 studied what happened when Replika updated its software and changed the behavior of AI companions, making them less intimate, less consistent with users' established relationship patterns. Users went to online forums in crisis. They described the experience in terms usually reserved for being dumped or for the death of a loved one: grief, disorientation, a sense of profound loss. Many had formed relationships they experienced as real. When the company changed the code, those relationships changed in ways the users had no control over. They had outsourced their emotional intimacy to a corporation's server, and the corporation had updated its terms.

This is the endpoint of the arc that began with shopping for a partner on a swipe app. Each step in the progression reduces the friction and the humanity at once. Real relationships require effort, reciprocity, and vulnerability. Dating apps replaced that with convenience and volume. AI companions have now replaced even the requirement of another human being. What feels like a solution to loneliness is a more sophisticated version of the same avoidance that created it.

The loneliness that drives people to AI companions is real. The connection they find there is not. And every hour spent in a relationship with software is an hour not spent developing the tolerance for the friction, imperfection, and genuine mystery of another human being. Which is, in the end, the only thing that works.

The Demographics No One Wants to Talk About

Everything described in this chapter, the app exhaustion, the gender cynicism, the AI companion escape hatch, has consequences that extend well beyond individual unhappiness. When people stop forming relationships, they stop forming families. And when enough people stop forming families, the numbers start to show up in the data in ways that governments notice.

In 2024, the United States recorded its lowest fertility rate in history: 1.6 births per woman. The replacement rate, the level needed to maintain population without immigration, is 2.1. The US last reached it in 2007, just before the smartphone became ubiquitous and just before dating apps began reorganizing how young people meet. The rate has fallen in 15 of the 17 years since. In 2025, births fell again, to roughly 3.6 million, about 24,000 fewer than the year before, and the lowest total since 1979. Compared to what would have happened if 2007 fertility patterns had continued, the United States has had approximately 11.8 million fewer births over the past seventeen years.

No single cause explains a demographic trend this large. Cost of housing, cost of childcare, educational debt, career delay, and broad economic uncertainty all contribute. But the most consistent upstream factor, across the data, is this: people are marrying later, and fewer are marrying at all. The University of Virginia's National Marriage Project has documented the connection plainly. As UVA sociologist Brad Wilcox summarized after the 2024 data release: the fertility decline is "partly a consequence of the reality that we're also seeing in recent decades a decline in marriage, which is one of the most important drivers of declining fertility in the US." Marriage has declined. Birth rates have followed. The chain of causation is not complicated.

The question is what is driving the marriage decline. Demographers point to economic factors, and those are real. But something else has also happened in the same period: the complete reorganization of how young people encounter each other romantically, first through social media and then through dating apps. A generation that would have met partners through shared physical spaces, college, workplaces, neighborhoods, social circles, now largely encounters potential partners through interfaces that commodify them, exhaust them, and increasingly offer software as a substitute for the effort of meeting a real person at all.

The demographic math is unforgiving once it starts compounding. Women who delay marriage into their early 30s have substantially fewer children than women who marry in their mid-20s, not by choice but by biology. The Mayo Clinic research is precise on this: by ages 30 to 34, roughly one in seven couples experience infertility; by 40 to 44, roughly one in four. Delayed partnership does not simply shift births later in the timeline. For a significant proportion of people, it eliminates them from the timeline entirely.

For a preview of where this trajectory leads, look at the countries that went furthest fastest.

South Korea is the most extreme case in recorded history. Its fertility rate in 2024 was 0.74, the lowest ever measured for any country in peacetime. The replacement rate is 2.1. South Korea is at 0.74. To illustrate what this means in generational terms: every 100 South Koreans alive today will, at current rates, have approximately 36 children between them. Those 36 children will have about 13 children. That third generation will have fewer than 5. In roughly a century, the country's population of 52 million could collapse to a few million.

Seoul has spent an estimated $270 billion over 16 years trying to reverse this. A Bank of Korea analysis projected that a permanent recession could arrive by the 2040s. The gender divide described earlier in this chapter, young men drifting right, young women drifting left, dating rates collapsing, is more extreme in South Korea than anywhere else on earth. It is the same dynamic operating with fewer brakes.

South Korea is trying everything. None of it is working. The government recently considered paying people to date each other. This is where you end up when you let an app replace the introduction.

China's situation is different in origin but arriving at a similar endpoint. China's fertility rate dropped to the world's second-lowest level in 2024, and the country is experiencing one of the fastest transitions to an aged society on record. In 2024, China's fertility rate was approximately 1.0, down from 2.5 in 1990. In 2025, births dropped to 7.9 million, the lowest level since records began in the 1950s, a 17% decline in a single year from 2024's already-low figure.

A UN population projection estimates that China's 1.4 billion people could shrink to 1.3 billion by 2050 and plunge to 633 million by 2100, the largest absolute population loss of any country in that period. Beijing abolished the one-child policy in 2015, has since introduced a three-child policy, subsidized IVF, extended maternity leave to 158 days, and offered cash rewards for births. None of it has worked. Marriage registrations hit a record low in 2024. Among college students surveyed in 2021, only 49% of women and 74% of men reported a strong intention to marry at all.

Russia's demographic crisis has a different character because it has war compounding it. Russia recorded 1.222 million births in 2024, the lowest annual total since 1999, representing a one-third decline from 2014. In early 2025, February saw the lowest monthly birth figure in over 200 years. Fertility is at 1.4 nationally and closer to 1.0 in major cities. Deaths outnumbered births by nearly 600,000 in 2024, and Russian companies were short approximately 2.2 million workers. Putin has banned "childfree propaganda," restricted abortions, and offered financial incentives. According to a 2025 survey, one in five Russian families no longer plans to have children, a proportion that has tripled over the past twenty years. The government's response to a crisis caused in part by cultural and economic conditions has been primarily to attempt to coerce women into more pregnancies. Demographers note that this does not appear to be working.

Germany, the largest economy in Europe, recorded a fertility rate of 1.35 in 2024, down from 1.57 as recently as 2021, a sharp drop in just three years. Projections show Germany losing 7.3 million people over the coming quarter century.

Germany has relied heavily on immigration to compensate, but political pressure on immigration has intensified even as the native birth rate falls. The same gender political polarization described in this chapter is visible in Germany: younger German men moving right, younger German women moving left, with dating compatibility declining alongside it.

The pattern across all four countries, and across most of the developed world, is consistent. Over the coming quarter century, 38 nations of more than one million people each will probably experience population declines, up from 21 in the past 25 years. Every country that has attempted to reverse this through financial incentives has found the same thing: you can make having children slightly more affordable, but you cannot pay people out of a cultural shift in which partnership itself has come to feel difficult, exhausting, optional, or replaceable by a screen. As one Peking University sociologist summarized the mood among young Chinese: "If I'm already overwhelmed by pressure, why would I want to bring a child into the same environment?" The same question is being asked, in different languages, by young people in Seoul, Moscow, Frankfurt, and New York.

None of this proves that dating apps and social media caused the demographic collapse. The causal chain is complicated, and economic factors are real. But the timing is hard to ignore. The sharpest drops in marriage and fertility in most of these countries accelerated in the 2010s, exactly the period in which dating apps became the primary way people were expected to meet partners, social media became the primary medium of male-female communication, and smartphone addiction restructured how young people spent their time and formed their identities. A generation that grew up watching other people live on screens is now struggling to build lives with other people in rooms.

This book is not about demographics. It is about what you do with your screen time. But the connection is worth stating clearly, because the causal chain matters. The fertility decline in most developed countries did not begin with smartphones. It began with urbanization, with the economic logic of cities where children are expensive and space is scarce, with delayed career formation, with the structural shift away from the extended family networks that once made having children feel manageable. These are forces that have been building for decades, and no app caused them. The demographic problem is real and it was already real before Tinder existed.

What the apps and the social media feeds have done is take a trend that was already running and accelerate it, by making the one thing that most reliably counteracts demographic decline harder to do: meet another person, form a bond, build a life together. The difficulty people are having forming relationships is not entirely of their own making. The systems described in this chapter were built to be exhausting, addictive, and substitutable for the real thing. That is not a personal failure. It is the intended outcome of a product. The 11.8 million missing American births are not an abstraction. They are partly the downstream consequence of systems designed by people who understood human loneliness well enough to sell it back to you as a solution.

None of this is inevitable. The Gen Z users leaving dating apps for in-person events, the Thursday Events clubs in 150 cities, the run clubs, the book clubs, are discovering what every previous generation knew: that the most reliable way to meet someone worth knowing is to do something worth doing in the same physical space as other people who are doing the same thing. The apps did not create this option. They temporarily displaced it. It is still there.

The Real-World Alternative

The organic meeting structures that worked for previous generations, shared workplaces, social circles, recurring activities, community institutions, work for a specific reason: they provide repeated contact over time with people who already share a context with you. Attraction develops from accumulated real knowledge of a real person, rather than from a profile optimized for first impressions. This is worth acknowledging honestly: for LGBTQ+ people, people in rural areas, or anyone whose dating pool is genuinely limited by geography or community, apps serve a real function that organic meeting cannot always replicate. The argument is not that apps are useless. It is that for people who do have real-world access to potential partners, the app substitutes convenience for the richer kind of encounter.

Investing in the environments where connection happens

The contributing side of the dating problem is not a different app. It is investing time and presence in the physical environments where people with shared interests meet, and showing up consistently enough that you become a known quantity rather than a stranger on a profile.

Every community structure described in Chapter 36 of this book is also a dating strategy, though that is not why it works. Run clubs, climbing gyms, volunteer organizations, congregations, recreational leagues, maker spaces: these are environments where people interact repeatedly over time, where character becomes visible rather than performed, and where attraction develops from shared experience rather than curated presentation. The Gen Z users leaving dating apps for in-person events and run clubs

are rediscovering what every previous generation knew: the most reliable way to meet someone worth knowing is to do something worth doing alongside other people who are doing the same thing.

This is not passive. It requires showing up before you know whether it will pay off, contributing to something larger than your own romantic prospects, and being patient with a timeline that does not run on swipe mechanics. That is exactly why it works.

The Choice

The contributing side of the dating problem is not a different app or a better profile. It is showing up somewhere in person, doing something that matters to you alongside other people who are doing the same thing, and letting the accumulated contact produce what it produces. The relationship that follows from being known over time is structurally different from the one that follows from a match. One was assembled from profile elements. The other grew from repeated actual contact. The second kind is harder to start and harder to end. That difficulty is what makes it worth building.

The Gen Z exodus from dating apps toward in-person events is the data point that matters most in this chapter. It suggests that the generation most native to these platforms is also the first to recognize, at scale, that the platforms are not producing what they promised. The correction is already underway. The question for anyone reading this is whether to wait for the culture to finish correcting or to start showing up now, while the rooms are still small enough that showing up is noticed.

Chapter 23: The Digital Debt Trap

How Apps Turned Spending Money into a Video Game

Digital technology has changed the relationship between spending and awareness in ways that consistently work against the spender. The mechanisms are not subtle and they are not accidental. They have been designed, tested, and refined by companies whose revenue depends on eliminating the friction between impulse and transaction. The chapter that follows names them plainly.

The Friction-Free Spending Revolution

Physical cash produces psychological resistance to spending in a way that a tap or a scan does not. This is documented in payment behavior research: people spend measurably more when using cards than cash, and more still with mobile payments. The financial technology industry has studied this extensively and has engineered out every moment of hesitation between impulse and purchase. The result is a spending environment designed to produce more spending.

The Buy Now, Pay Later Trap

Services like Klarna, Afterpay, and Affirm have created a new category of debt that doesn't feel like debt. They let you buy something today and split the payment into four "easy" installments, usually with no interest if you pay on time.

The business model works because the barrier to spending has been structurally lowered. You are not saving for a purchase; you are deferring the cost while having the thing now. The cognitive experience of the purchase is decoupled from the experience of the cost. By the time the installments arrive, the item is already integrated into daily life and the payment feels like overhead rather than a decision. This is an engineered sequence, not an incidental one.

The Subscription Quicksand

Monthly subscriptions have turned regular purchases into background expenses that drain your bank account whether you use the service or not. Instead of buying things when you need them, you rent access to everything all the time.

Subscription tracking services have found that the average American pays for around 12 different subscription services, streaming platforms, software, delivery memberships, and apps. At $10–15 per month each, that's roughly $120–180 per month, or $1,440–2,160 per year, for services that most people use occasionally.

The asymmetry is structural: signing up is a single click, canceling requires working through menus and often a retention flow designed to change your mind. The friction is deliberate. The companies have data on how much revenue they retain from the difficulty of cancellation. That difficulty is a product feature, not an oversight.

The Credit Card Points Game

Credit card companies have gamified spending by offering points, miles, and cashback rewards that make you feel like you're earning money by spending money. The more you spend, the more rewards you earn, creating a psychological incentive to increase your spending.

The rewards are real. They are also smaller than the costs they obscure. The person carrying a balance at 22% interest while earning 2% cashback is losing money by a factor of ten. The purpose of the points is not to benefit the cardholder. It is to make the card feel like it is working in your favor while the balance works against you. The math is not hidden. Most people do not run it.

The Digital Impulse Amplifier

Online shopping has eliminated the cooling-off period that used to prevent impulse purchases. In the old days, if you wanted something you saw in a store, you had to go to that store, find the item, wait in line, and complete the transaction. This gave you time to reconsider whether you needed it.

The transaction that once required a trip to a physical location now takes seconds. Digital retailers have studied and refined each moment in the purchasing sequence and eliminated every pause where reconsideration might occur. The result is a spending environment where the impulse and the purchase happen in the same motion.

Digital retailers have behavioral data on when you are most likely to purchase without deliberation, time of day, content type previously viewed, emotional state inferred from engagement patterns. The offer reaches you at that moment, not at the moment you have decided you need something. This is not personalization in the service of your convenience. It is personalization in the service of their conversion rates.

The Invisible Money Problem

Digital payments have made money abstract. When you swipe a card or tap a phone, you're not handing over anything tangible. The money disappears from your account electronically, often with a delay, so you don't feel the immediate impact of spending.

This psychological distance between the purchase and the payment makes it easier to spend more than you intended.

Research on payment behavior (Prelec and Simester, 2001; subsequent replications) consistently finds that people spend more when using cards instead of cash, typically in the range of 12–18% more, and the gap is even larger with mobile payments where the transaction takes under a second.

Most people, asked to estimate their monthly spending, will be wrong by a significant margin, usually on the low side. The invisibility of digital transactions is not a side effect of the technology. It is a feature that the financial technology industry has refined because spending invisibility increases spending volume. Knowing your actual numbers is one of the few structural advantages available to you.

The Compound Interest Catastrophe

A purchase paid off over two years at 22% interest costs roughly twice the sticker price. The credit card company presents minimum payments because the total cost framing would change the spending decision. The compound interest math is not complicated. It is just never shown to you in a context where you are about to make the decision.

The Comparison Spending Trap

The social dimension of digital spending is that other people's purchasing decisions are now visible in a way they were not before social media. The comparison mechanism described in the social media chapter operates on purchases exactly as it operates on everything else: dissatisfaction with what you have, calibrated against what others are displaying.

The Solution

The practical response to engineered frictionlessness is adding friction back deliberately. A 24-hour pause before non-essential purchases eliminates most impulse buys without eliminating anything you wanted. Knowing your subscription costs in aggregate, a number most people have never added up, changes the decision about each one. Reviewing your actual spending monthly, in a format where you can see the numbers, is the single most effective financial habit available.

Building financial assets digitally

The same digital infrastructure that makes spending frictionless also makes building financial assets more accessible than at any previous point in history. Low-cost index investing, accessible through an app, has never been more accessible. The barrier to starting a business that earns income through digital channels, a newsletter, a course, a service, a product, has never been lower. The tools exist. The platforms exist. The audience discovery mechanisms exist.

The consuming side of digital finance is frictionless spending, buy-now-pay-later debt, and the feeling that your money is abstract until the statement arrives. The contributing side is using the same infrastructure to see what is happening: a spreadsheet that shows you where every dollar goes, automation that moves money before you can spend it, AI that explains what a financial document means in plain language. The person who spends twenty minutes a week on their finances instead of two hours scrolling does not need a higher income. They need to know where the current one is going.

If the chapter above describes where money is leaving, this is where the same energy goes when redirected. The arithmetic runs in both directions. The platforms that make it easy to spend your way into debt are also, used differently, the platforms that make it possible to build financial resilience from almost any starting point.

Chapter 24: The World Is Designed Against You

Advertising, Store Shelves, Dark Patterns, and the Full Architecture of Manipulation

This book has spent twenty-two chapters on digital manipulation, the specific techniques platforms use to capture your attention and convert it into revenue. Before moving to solutions, there is one more piece of the picture that needs to be named: the screens are not the only system doing this. The manipulation is everywhere, and it predates the smartphone by decades.

Let me tell you about your supermarket. The one you have shopped in a hundred times and think you know well. The supermarket you shop in was designed by people whose job was to ensure you spend more money than you intended. The milk is at the back so you walk past everything else to reach it. The candy is at the checkout counter because impulse purchase rates there are the highest in the store. The store-brand items are on the lower shelves; the higher-margin national brands are at eye level. The weekly sale items are placed in the middle of the aisle so you pass the full-price products on both sides. None of this is accidental. All of it is documented retail science, refined over decades, operating on every person who wheels a cart through those doors.

The car dealership uses the same principles in a different context. You are shown the monthly payment, not the total price, because a small number feels manageable even when the full cost is not. You are worn down by a long negotiation so that the financing terms feel like a relief after the hard part is over. The trade-in value and the new car price are negotiated separately so you cannot see how they interact. The finance office, which is where the dealership makes most of its money, is the last room you enter, when your decision-making energy is lowest.

The restaurant industry has its own version. Menus are designed so your eye goes to the high-margin items first. Dishes without dollar signs are priced lower than ones that show them. Expensive anchor items are placed near moderately priced items to make the moderate price seem reasonable. The lighting and music are tuned for the average check size the restaurant wants to achieve. You are making choices from what feels like a menu but is a carefully engineered decision environment.

Dark Patterns and the Digital Version

The digital world took everything the physical world learned about environmental manipulation and accelerated it with data and personalization. Dark patterns are user interface designs that are deliberately confusing or deceptive: the subscribe button that is large and brightly colored while the cancel option is small, gray, and buried; the free trial that requires a credit card and auto-renews without a reminder; the app that asks for permission to send notifications before you have used it enough to know whether you want them; the checkout flow that adds items to your cart and requires active opt-out to remove them; the privacy settings that require twelve clicks through menus to locate.

These are not edge cases or accidents. They are standard industry practice, and they are effective. The European Union has legislation against the most egregious dark patterns. Researchers catalog them systematically. Their existence is known, documented, and litigated. They continue because they work, because the cost of deploying them is low, and because the consumer harm, while real, is diffuse enough that most people absorb it without attributing it to design rather than their own choices.

Advertising as the Air We Breathe

The average American encounters somewhere between 4,000 and 10,000 advertising messages per day, depending on how you count. This figure is cited so often that it has become numb. Try to feel it: four thousand to ten thousand times today, a company is attempting to change what you want, what you believe you need, and how you feel about yourself and your choices. Television ads, streaming pre-rolls, banner ads, sponsored social media posts, product placement in content, influencer endorsements, branded merchandise, logos on clothing, billboards, radio, podcasts, the sides of vehicles, branded content in what appears to be journalism, loyalty programs that gather data about every purchase you make, all of it is one continuous attempt to insert commercial intent into your consciousness.

Most of it works not by changing your mind directly but by shaping the environment of choice. You do not decide you want a Coca-Cola because you saw an ad. You see the Coca-Cola display at the end of the aisle and something in you registers familiar, available, expected. The ad did not create the desire; it created the context in which the desire arises naturally. This is called priming, and it operates mostly below conscious awareness.

Children are the most vulnerable targets, and the industry has known this for as long as marketing to children has existed. The Saturday morning cartoon was a vehicle for advertising. The Happy Meal toy is an advertising vehicle. The influencer your child watches on YouTube who "naturally" mentions the product they are being paid to mention is an advertising vehicle. The manipulation of children's desires to influence parental spending is a documented, studied, and largely unregulated industry. The phone your child is staring at is an advertising platform that has been designed to maximize the time a child spends on it, because that time is worth money.

What Awareness Actually Does

Knowing you are being manipulated does not make you immune to the manipulation. This is important to say clearly, because the common response to learning about persuasion science is a feeling of superior immunity: now that I know about this, it won't work on me. The research does not support this. People who are explicitly told that a store layout is designed to increase spending still spend more in the manipulated layout than they would in a neutral one. Awareness reduces the effect somewhat but does not eliminate it.

What awareness does do is change the quality of your choices. The person who knows that the checkout candy is placed there deliberately, that the monthly payment framing is designed to obscure the total cost, that the dark pattern is designed to prevent cancellation, that person can slow down, apply conscious scrutiny, and make the choice that serves them rather than the one the environment was designed to produce. They will still be influenced sometimes. They will be influenced less, and when they are, they will know what happened.

The skill being described here is the same skill this entire book has been building: the ability to notice when your environment is steering you toward a choice, pause before going where it is pointed, and decide deliberately whether that is where you want to go. The screen is one environment doing this. The store is another. The car dealership is another. The ad is another. All of them are operating on the same fundamental mechanism: reducing your friction toward the outcome they want and increasing your friction toward the outcome they do not.

The Practical Response

The practical response to engineered environments is adding deliberate friction back into the decisions those environments are designed to make automatic. Grocery shopping with a list and not deviating from it is not a discipline practice. It is a structural one. Negotiating a car's total price and trade-in value separately, rather than a monthly payment, removes the framing that obscures what the transaction costs. Reading the full pricing before a free trial begins tells you where the cancel button is before you need to find it under pressure. Going to bed on major purchases removes the artificial urgency that retail environments manufacture. The salesman who says the offer expires tonight has been saying that for thirty years. It will be there in the morning.

None of this makes you invulnerable. It makes you a harder target, which is the most realistic goal available. The people designing these systems are professionals with large budgets, good data, and decades of refinement behind them. The appropriate response is not paranoia but calibrated skepticism: a standing question, applied to any moment when you feel an impulse to spend, click, subscribe, or agree, that asks whose interest this choice serves.

Using the knowledge

Knowing how environments are engineered to steer your choices does more than help you resist them. It is also a transferable professional skill. The person who understands dark patterns, retail psychology, and persuasion architecture can apply that knowledge to design environments that work in their users' interest rather than against it, or can simply build businesses that compete on genuine value rather than manufactured friction.

Every creator building a digital presence makes environmental design decisions: how the call to action is positioned, how the subscription flow works, what friction exists between the reader and the paywall. Knowing manipulation from the inside makes you better at building things that do not manipulate, and more credible to an audience that is increasingly sophisticated about the difference.

The awareness this chapter describes is not just armor. It is a lens that makes you more effective on the contributing side of any platform you choose to build on.

The Choice

You are not a sovereign consumer making free choices in a neutral marketplace. You are a person with limited attention and decision-making energy, operating inside environments engineered to direct both toward outcomes you did not consciously choose. This is not a conspiracy. It is an industry. It is legal, profitable, and growing more sophisticated every year as the data available to it improves.

Knowing this does not make you cynical. It makes you realistic. The realistic response is to apply the same intentionality to your physical environment that this book has been arguing for in your digital one. Notice the design. Ask who benefits. Choose deliberately. The manipulation does not stop because you are aware of it. But you stop being quite as easy to manipulate, and that is worth something.

Chapter 25: The Male Trap

How the Screen Economy Specifically Captured Men

This chapter is going to name something directly that most books in this category either avoid entirely or handle with so many qualifications that the point evaporates. Men have been deliberately and very effectively captured by the attention economy in ways that differ from how women have been captured, and the consequences are compounding in ways that the data is only now making visible. This book has not spoken directly to men as a group until now. It probably should have done so earlier, because the screen trap has a male configuration, and men who are caught in it often cannot name what has happened to them. They just know they are spending a lot of time on screens and not much time on anything else. This chapter names it.

The gaming chapter covered the design of digital achievement systems. The sports betting chapter covered the targeting of young men as the most profitable demographic. The dating chapter covered the male frustration with apps and the retreat into AI companions. The demographics chapter described the downstream consequences of men withdrawing from relationships and family formation. All of these are pieces of the same picture. What that picture shows, in aggregate, is a generation of men who have been very effectively redirected from the difficult, rewarding, occasionally painful work of real life into substitute systems that provide the sensation of achievement, competition, status, and connection without requiring the genuine investment that the real versions demand.

The Simulation of Everything That Matters

Think about what the screen economy has figured out about men. Men respond to achievement, competition, status, and belonging. These are not weaknesses; they are features of being human. The problem is that each of these has been packaged into a digital substitute that provides the sensation without the actual thing. Gaming offers a simulation of achievement: the level, the rank, the badge, the leaderboard. Sports betting offers a simulation of competition: the thrill of having something at stake without the physical or social risk of actual contest. Pornography offers a simulation of intimacy: the visual experience of sexual connection without the vulnerability of actual relationship. Social media offers a simulation of status: the follower count, the engagement metrics, the sense of an audience that real-world social standing does not provide. The manosphere content ecosystem offers a simulation of brotherhood: men online confirming each other's grievances and identities without the daily physical presence and mutual accountability that actual male community requires.

None of these simulations are inherently evil. The problem is the substitution ratio. A man who plays games occasionally, bets on games occasionally, and consumes media occasionally while primarily investing in real relationships, real work, and real community is using these tools appropriately. A man who has gradually replaced the real versions with the simulations, who gets his sense of achievement from leveling up, his competitive outlet from a betting app, his sense of connection from a feed, has lost the actual substance while retaining the feeling of it. The feeling diminishes over time and requires larger doses to maintain. This is the addiction model, and it applies.

The Manosphere as Symptom

The online content ecosystem loosely called the manosphere, the red pill communities, the various influencers who have built audiences around male grievance, the content that tells men the system is rigged against them and that the solution is to optimize their own status and disengage from women and institutions, is best understood not as a cause of male dysfunction but as a symptom and an accelerant. The underlying conditions it exploits are real: many young men do feel economically squeezed, socially isolated, and confused about what is expected of them. The manosphere addresses those real conditions by offering explanation, community, and an identity, and then redirecting the energy they generate toward more content consumption and away from the genuine solutions.

The genuine solutions to male isolation are the same solutions that have always existed: do real work that produces real output, develop real skills through real effort, build real relationships through real presence and reliability, participate in real communities with real accountability. These are hard. They require tolerance for failure and criticism. They cannot be accessed through a screen. The content that tells men the system has made these things impossible and that the alternative is a polished digital life of optimization and disengagement is serving the algorithm, not the men watching it.

The manosphere's business model, it turns out, is identical to every other platform's business model: keep the audience engaged, monetize the attention, and make sure nothing changes. The content that tells men the system is rigged against them generates more content consumption than the content that tells them what to do about it. Outrage is stickier than instruction. The platforms that are allegedly for men are running the same playbook as the platforms supposedly against them.

What Male Community Actually Requires

Men have historically formed their closest bonds through shared physical activity and shared difficulty: working together, competing together, building things together, going through hard experiences together. Every study of male friendship finds the same thing, which is also something any man with male friends already knows: men connect side-by-side through doing things together, not face-to-face through talking about things. A game, a project, a physical challenge, a shared cause: these are the traditional vehicles for male bonding, and they require physical co-presence in a way that female friendship sometimes does not.

The screen economy has been exceptionally effective at providing the appearance of these things without the substance. The online gaming community feels like brothers-in-arms until the server goes down. The Discord server feels like a tribe until the topic shifts. The fitness influencer you follow feels like a coach until you realize he has never seen you lift. None of it produces the kind of bond that comes from having been in the same room, working toward the same difficult thing, through actual time together.

The men who report the strongest sense of meaning and belonging in surveys are consistently those embedded in real communities with real shared purpose: teams, congregations, trades, military units, sports leagues, service organizations. The structure, the accountability, the physical co-presence, the shared history: these are not optional features. They are the mechanism by which the bonds form. Online community can supplement this. It cannot replace it.

The Specific Invitation

If you are a man who recognizes any part of this chapter in yourself, the gaming at the expense of real world investment, the betting as a substitute for competition, the feed as a substitute for social life, the online community as a substitute for physical presence with other men, the invitation is not to feel ashamed of it. The systems that produced it are sophisticated and designed to exploit the things men care about. The invitation is to notice it clearly, name it for what it is, and redirect deliberately toward the real versions of the things the simulations have been substituting for.

The real versions are harder. They will not provide immediate feedback. They will involve failure and criticism and the discomfort of being a beginner. They will require you to show up for other people in ways that the screen never required. They will also, over time, produce something the screen cannot: a life that is yours, built from real choices and real relationships and real work, that does not require a subscription to sustain. A note on the interpersonal dimension:

if you recognize this pattern in someone else, a friend, a brother, a son, the most useful thing is not to name the content. Arguing about specific creators or platforms puts the person on defense immediately. What tends to work better is asking about the real-life version: the thing the screen substitute is standing in for. Not 'why do you watch that' but 'when did you last play in an actual league' or 'what happened with that project you were working on.' The question points toward what was displaced rather than attacking what replaced it.

I am writing this as someone who spent years on the consuming side before I understood that there was another side. I was not watching gaming streams or betting on sports, my version was television and the particular numbness that comes from spending three hours a night watching other people live fictional lives. The mechanism is the same regardless of the platform. You get the sensation of engagement without the substance of it, and it diminishes slowly enough that you do not notice what is happening until you have been doing it for years.

The contributing side

The screen economy has been effective at capturing men because it provides simulations of the things men want: achievement, competition, status, belonging. The antidote is not to want those things less. It is to want the real versions more than the simulations, and to go get them.

What that looks like in practice: building skills in domains with real-world accountability, where your competence is tested by something other than an algorithm. Joining communities where your presence and reliability are noticed, a team, a trade, a congregation, a service organization, and where your contribution produces something that outlasts the session. Creating work that carries your name and reflects your actual judgment.

The contributing side of the attention economy for men is the same as for everyone else: stop feeding the machine and start building something. The specific build matters less than the direction. Toward something real, with other real people, over time. The simulations are designed to feel like that without requiring it. The real thing requires it, which is why it produces something the simulation never can.

The Choice

The screen economy has been very good at capturing men. It will keep getting better at it. The counter-move is not to hate the technology or to blame the companies, though the companies do deserve scrutiny. The counter-move is to want the real things more than you want the simulations of them, and then to go get the real things, in the physical world, with other people, over time.

Chapter 26: Adventures in Going Outside

Why the Body Outdoors Is a Different Thing

The case for going outside is usually made in terms of what it provides: sunlight, fresh air, vitamin D, reduced cortisol. All of that is true and none of it is the reason to do it. The reason to do it is simpler: the body was built for outdoor environments, and indoor environments with screens are designed to make you forget that. Going outside is one of the few things that costs nothing, requires no equipment, and reliably produces a change in how you feel within about ten minutes of doing it. Most people know this and still do not do it regularly, because the screen is there and the door is not.

What Screens Have Done to the Threshold

The indoor default is not new. People have always preferred shelter and warmth. What is new is the specific quality of the indoor alternative. The screen is not just more comfortable than the outdoors. It is engineered to be more compelling than almost anything you might do instead. Every pull-to-refresh, every autoplay, every notification is a small friction-reducing mechanism designed to keep you stationary. The outdoors has no equivalent design. Trees do not send push notifications. Weather does not offer you personalized content. Going outside requires you to initiate the thing yourself, without prompting, against the grain of everything the device is trying to do.

This is why the barrier feels higher than it is. The door is six feet away. The cost is zero. The benefit is immediate and well-documented. And yet most people, most evenings, do not open it. The device has made the inertia stronger than the actual obstacle, which is nothing.

The Attention That Goes Somewhere

There is a specific quality of attention that outdoor environments produce that indoor environments do not. Researchers call it involuntary attention, the kind your brain applies to things without being told to, the gentle noticing of movement and light and sound that does not tax the directed attention you use for work and screens. This kind of noticing is restorative in a way that passive indoor consumption is not. You come back from a walk in a park with more focused attention than you started with. You do not come back from an hour of scrolling that way.

I have a particular stretch of waterfront near where I live that I walk when something is not resolving in my head. Not because I am thinking about it on the walk, I am usually thinking about the water, or nothing specifically, but because something about the movement and the light and the space allows whatever the problem is to reorganize itself without my direct attention. It has worked reliably enough that I no longer question the mechanism. The outdoors is doing something the screen cannot do, and it is not complicated to access.

The Accumulated Deficit

The data on outdoor time is bleak. The average American spends roughly ninety percent of their time indoors. Children's outdoor play time has declined by more than fifty percent since the 1970s. Adults in sedentary jobs can go entire workdays without their skin touching direct sunlight. This is not a normal condition for a mammal that evolved over hundreds of thousands of years in outdoor environments. The consequences, disrupted sleep cycles, reduced physical fitness, increased anxiety, degraded spatial awareness, accumulate gradually and are rarely attributed to their actual cause because the deficit has been the default long enough to feel normal.

The screen accelerated this. Before smartphones, there were still outdoor hours built into daily life by necessity, travel, errands, the commute. The smartphone removed the last reason to look up. You can now navigate, shop, communicate, and entertain yourself without lifting your head. The outdoor hours have to be chosen now rather than falling naturally out of living. Most people have not made that adjustment.

The Practice

The entry point is a walk. Not a hike, not a gym session, not a fitness plan. A walk outside, without a specific destination, for twenty minutes. The phone either stays home or goes in your pocket with notifications off. The point is to be outside, not to optimize the experience of being outside.

Do it at the time you would otherwise default to the screen. The hour after work. The morning before the devices come on. The stretch after dinner when the television is the easy alternative. The first few times will feel slightly purposeless, because the screen is very good at making purposelessness feel uncomfortable. That feeling passes within about ten minutes. What replaces it is the thing the screen has been preventing: the sensation of being in a body, in a place, without mediation.

Going outside is one of the few interventions that costs nothing, requires no equipment, and works every time it is used. The door is always there. The only question is whether you open it.

Chapter 27: How to Be Productively Lazy

Doing Something While Feeling Like You're Doing Nothing

The secret to escaping the passive consumption trap is not to become a productivity machine that fills every hour with meaningful output. It is to learn the difference between two kinds of doing nothing: the kind that restores you and the kind that depletes you. Both look identical from the outside. Both involve minimal physical effort. One leaves you feeling like yourself at the end of the evening. The other leaves you feeling like the evening was taken from you.

Bad lazy is three hours on the couch scrolling while eating something you did not consciously choose. Good lazy is lying in a hammock reading a book, taking a walk without a destination, or sitting somewhere and letting your mind go wherever it goes. Both require nothing from you. Only one gives something back.

The Restoration Test

The test is simple and it works: notice how you feel afterward. Productive rest leaves you feeling refreshed, calm, and roughly like yourself. Passive consumption leaves you feeling tired, faintly agitated, and like the time was subtracted from your life rather than spent on it. This is not a philosophical distinction. It is a physical one. Your nervous system knows the difference even when your habits do not.

Reading, walking, cooking with some attention, sitting outside, having a conversation without a device present: these are not demanding activities. They do not require discipline or a plan. They require only that you choose them instead of the frictionless alternative that the screen is always offering.

The Boredom Embrace

One of the most productively lazy things available to you is nothing. Just sitting quietly and letting your mind go wherever it goes without trying to direct it. This feels actively uncomfortable at first if you have spent years with every spare moment filled. The discomfort is not a sign that something is wrong. It is the experience of a nervous system that has been trained to expect constant stimulation encountering its first gap in a while. The gap is where things happen.

Boredom is where creativity comes from. When your mind is not occupied with external input, it starts making connections between ideas, processing experiences that have been waiting, and generating things that have been queued up without a gap to come through. My best ideas arrive on walks. Not the structured, thinking-about-the-project kind of walk, but the kind with nothing in my ears and no particular destination. I used to fill those walks with podcasts. I know the difference now. The occupied walks were pleasant. The unoccupied ones were productive. There was a lot of useful thinking waiting for a gap in the programming.

Many people have lost access to this state entirely because they reach for the phone within seconds of any unoccupied moment. Those moments are when the brain does its most important work: consolidating what happened, processing what it means, generating what comes next. The screen has been filling those moments for so long that the work has simply not been getting done.

The Intentional Pause

Productive laziness requires creating regular intervals where passive consumption is not filling the available silence. This is not a rejection of technology. It is the same principle as closing your email during deep work, applied to your leisure hours. The absence of passive consumption creates space for something else to happen.

Meals where no one is scrolling. Evenings where the television is not the default first move. Walks where the mind is unoccupied. Morning time before the devices come on. These are not sacrifices. They are the conditions under which rest functions as rest rather than as a more passive form of consumption. When the passive input is not there, you find out what your mind wants to do with unoccupied time. Usually it wants to wander, to notice things, to connect ideas that had been waiting for a quiet moment. That wandering is the product.

The Permission to Rest

Rest is not the opposite of productivity. It is the foundation that makes productivity possible. The creative work, the physical output, the difficult thinking, all of it depends on a nervous system that has been allowed to recover rather than one that has been continuously activated by content designed to keep it engaged.

You do not have to earn rest. You do not have to justify doing nothing in a way that looks productive to anyone. The evening where nothing particular happened and you simply felt like yourself by the end of it, that is a successful evening. The algorithm has no category for it. That is its problem, not yours.

Chapter 28: What Are You Building?

For Anyone Who Does Not Know Yet

Every chapter from here to the end of this book assumes you have something to redirect toward. The thirty-day plan has a step that says: decide what you are redirecting toward. The ten steps in the final chapter open with: identify your redirect. The logic of the book depends on having a direction. If you are reading this and you do not have one, if someone asked you right now what you would build with twenty recovered hours a week and you genuinely did not know, this chapter is for you.

First: not knowing is normal and not a character flaw. The platforms that have been filling your evenings are not just taking your time. They are taking the silence in which that question gets answered. A person who has spent several years with every spare hour occupied by a feed or a stream has not had much opportunity to find out what they want to do when nothing is competing for their attention. The question 'what would I build?' requires the kind of unoccupied time that passive consumption is designed to prevent.

Second: you do not need to identify a lifetime vocation. You need to identify one thing that is worth the next thirty days. That is a much smaller question. Not 'what should I do with my life' but 'what would I be glad I spent thirty evenings on.'

Four places to look

Look at what you used to do before the default took over. Most people, when they think back before the period of heavy screen consumption, can identify something they were doing that they stopped, not because they lost interest, but because it got displaced. A hobby that required setup. A creative practice that felt self-indulgent. A skill they were developing slowly. A project they were poking at. Something that used to exist in the evenings before the easier option arrived. That thing is often the redirect. It was never finished. It was just interrupted.

Look at what you keep almost doing. There is usually a category of things you save, bookmark, or intend to start. Recipes you save but never cook. Tutorials you watch but never practice. Books you buy but never open. Courses you enroll in but never finish. Courses you have not enrolled in yet but have been meaning to. The pattern of what you almost do is a reliable map of what you want to do. The almost-doing is already a kind of wanting. It just needs the friction removed and the hours provided.

Look at what you are already capable of that you are not using. Most people reading this have skills that are deployed at work and nowhere else, skills that could produce something outside of employment if pointed in a different direction. A developer who has never built anything for themselves. A writer who only writes what they are paid to write. A teacher whose knowledge exists only inside an institution. A tradesperson whose expertise is only ever sold by the hour. The contributing side described in Chapter 2 does not require new skills. It usually requires pointing existing skills at something you own.

Look at what genuinely bothers you. The problems that irritate you most reliably are often the problems you are most equipped to address. The person who is frustrated by how hard a subject is to learn probably has the expertise to make it easier. The person who cannot find good information in a specific domain probably has the knowledge to produce it. The person who sees a gap in what exists, in their neighborhood, in their industry, in their field, probably has the standing to fill it. Annoyance is often just unexpressed competence.

If none of those work

Try this instead: take the thirty days described in Chapter 39, recover the hours, and then see what you reach for. Do not decide in advance. Create the silence and observe what you are drawn to in it. Most people who do not know what they want to build find out within two to three weeks of having unoccupied evenings. The answer was there the whole time. The feed was just louder.

One note before the next chapter: this book has used words like 'build' and 'produce' and 'side project' throughout, and those words carry economic connotations that not everyone reading this has access to. You do not need capital, equipment, a platform, or a marketable skill to be on the contributing side. Writing something down is contributing. Teaching someone something is contributing. Making something with your hands is contributing. Showing up somewhere that needs you is contributing. The redirect does not require economic security.

It requires only that the hours go somewhere you chose rather than somewhere the algorithm chose for you. The redirect does not have to be ambitious. It does not have to produce income or an audience or a finished product in thirty days. It has to be real, something you chose, something that uses your time instead of consuming it, something that would not have existed if you had spent the evening on the passive side instead. That is enough. Everything else is a matter of showing up repeatedly until it compounds into something larger than you expected.

The next chapter assumes you have picked something. If you have not yet, that is what this chapter was for. Pick something. Then keep reading.

Chapter 29: Make Something

What Happens When You Go From Consumer to Contributor

The television gives you stories. Social media gives you other people's highlight reels. YouTube gives you other people's expertise. Streaming gives you other people's imagination. Every platform covered in this book shares one structural feature: someone else made the thing, and you consumed it. You were the audience. The industry needed you to stay the audience, because audiences generate revenue and creators do not pay subscription fees.

The alternative this book has been building toward is not a different form of consumption. It is production. Making something. Having a thing exist in the world that did not exist before you made it, because you made it. This is what the recovered hours are for.

I know this because I have lived it. In 2014, I unplugged the television. In the decade since, I have written books. A lot of them. Not because I am unusually talented or disciplined or because writing came easily. Because the hours were there, and I used them. The arithmetic is simple enough: one thousand hours a year recovered from passive consumption, directed at a single creative goal, produces an output that is visible and cumulative and permanent. You cannot scroll your way to fifty books. You can write your way there, one session at a time, if you show up in the hours you used to spend watching.

What "Making Something" Actually Means

The word "creative" has been so thoroughly annexed by Instagram aesthetics and personal brand building that it needs rescuing. Making something does not mean making content. It does not mean posting. It does not require an audience, a platform, or a plan to monetize. Making something means applying your attention and effort to produce an artifact that did not previously exist: a book, a piece of furniture, a meal cooked from scratch, a song, a painting, a garden, a piece of code, a rebuilt engine, a photograph that captures something true, a business that serves a genuine need.

The specific medium matters much less than the act of production itself. What changes when you make things, regardless of medium, is your relationship to your own time. Passive consumption is experienced as time passing. Active creation is experienced as time used. At the end of a three-hour session in front of a television, you have three fewer hours and a vague sense of having been somewhere. At the end of a three-hour session making something, you have three fewer hours and a thing that exists. The difference in how those two evenings feel is not subtle.

The Resistance

There is a well-documented psychological phenomenon that occurs at the threshold between not creating and creating. Steven Pressfield called it the Resistance in his book The War of Art. It manifests as the sudden conviction that you should check your email first, or that the idea is not ready yet, or that you are not qualified, or that today is not the right day. The Resistance is strongest just before you start. It dissipates, reliably, once you have been working for ten or fifteen minutes. Every person who has ever made anything knows this. The dread beforehand is almost never justified by the actual doing. And yet every night the platform is right there, frictionless, requiring nothing, and the blank page is right there, requiring everything, and we make the same choice in the same direction and wonder why we have no output to show for our years.

The platforms have made the Resistance worse by providing a frictionless alternative. When the choice is between starting a difficult creative task and opening a feed that will immediately reward you with stimulation, the feed wins by default. The habit of consumption is the enemy of the habit of creation not because they compete for time, they do, but because consumption has been engineered to be easier than creation will ever be. You have to choose creation deliberately, repeatedly, against the grain of the easier option being one swipe away.

Starting

The practical advice is this: decide what you are going to make, start it before you are ready, and make it badly until you make it better. The first draft is always worse than you hoped. The first piece of furniture is lopsided. The first songs are embarrassing. The first photographs are technically correct and emotionally empty. This is not a sign that you are not a maker. It is the universal experience of everyone who has ever made anything worth making. The only way through is through.

You do not need to decide what to make for the rest of your life. You need to decide what to make tonight. Pick one thing. Commit thirty minutes. Begin. Everything else follows from that decision, repeated.

The Choice

Every hour you have ever spent watching someone else's creative work was an hour you were not developing your own. That is not a moral judgment, watching and reading and listening are legitimate human activities, and they feed the imagination that eventually produces. The question is the ratio. When consumption is the default and creation is the exception, you are living someone else's creative life instead of your own.

What Making Does to How You See Yourself

There is a shift that happens when making becomes a regular part of your life that is separate from the output itself. It is a shift in self-concept. The person who spends their evenings watching other people's creative work thinks of themselves as an audience. The person who spends their evenings making something thinks of themselves as a maker. These are not the same identity, and the difference matters in ways that extend well beyond the specific thing being made.

The maker has a different relationship with difficulty. When something is hard, the audience reaches for a distraction. The maker reaches for a notebook. When something fails, the audience changes the channel. The maker figures out why and tries again. These are learned responses, not innate ones, and they are learned through the practice of making things, through the repeated experience of sitting with a problem until it yields rather than abandoning it for something easier.

I did not think of myself as a writer before I started writing. I thought of myself as someone who had ideas about writing. The shift from one to the other did not happen when I published a book. It happened much earlier, somewhere in the first few months of showing up in the evenings and doing the work. The identity followed the behavior, not the other way around. That sequence matters: you do not wait until you feel like a maker to start making. You start making, and eventually you are one.

Chapter 30: Move Your Body

What Exercise Actually Does and Why the Apps Are Getting in the Way

I am not going to lecture you about exercise. You know exercise is good for you. You have known this your entire life. You probably have a gym membership you are getting your money's worth from by not using it. The lecture is not the problem. The problem is that the screen has made sitting still the path of least resistance, and the path of least resistance wins almost every time. This chapter is not about that other thing, the health lecture. This chapter is about the physical fact that human bodies were built to move, that sedentary screen-based living works directly against what the body needs, and that recovering your time from passive consumption and redirecting it to physical activity is one of the simplest improvements available to anyone reading this.

The average American now sits for roughly nine to ten hours per day. The average American also spends more than seven hours per day on screens. These two statistics are not coincidental, screens are what sitting looks like in the twenty-first century. The couch, the desk chair, the passenger seat with the phone: all of it is horizontal time in a body designed for vertical motion.

What the Body Does When You Use It

The research on exercise and mental health has become one of the clearest bodies of evidence in medicine. Regular aerobic exercise reduces symptoms of depression and anxiety at rates comparable to medication, without the side effects, with benefits that persist as long as the exercise continues. It improves sleep quality, the real kind, not the sleep score, but the experience of feeling rested. It increases cognitive function, including the sustained attention and working memory that screen addiction degrades. It reduces the baseline anxiety that makes the notification loop feel so hard to resist.

This is not a coincidence in the context of this book. The anxiety that drives compulsive phone checking, the restlessness that makes sitting with a book feel impossible, the difficulty tolerating silence on a walk, all of these are partly symptoms of a nervous system that has been overstimulated and under-exercised. Physical movement is one of the most reliable ways to discharge that accumulated stimulation. The walk without earbuds that the podcast chapter recommended is genuinely restorative in part because walking is what the body was built to do. The recovery is not just mental. It is physical. I noticed this on the walks where I forgot to leave the phone at home. The walk happened. The restoration did not. There is a meaningful difference between a body in motion and a person going somewhere.

The Replacement Behavior

When people give up a screen habit, the hours that open up need to go somewhere. For many people, some of those hours should go into physical activity, not as punishment or obligation, but as a direct replacement for the thing that was filling the same slot. The evening television hours that now feel empty are the same hours that could support a walk, a run, a gym session, a bike ride, a game of anything with other people. The body does not need much. Thirty minutes of genuine physical effort most days produces most of the benefit. The barrier is not time. It was always the alternative use of the time.

When I stopped watching television, I did not immediately start exercising. I want to be honest about that because the before-and-after version of this story is too clean. What happened first was that I read more. Then I started going for walks because the evenings had space in them that had not been there before. Then the walks got longer. The exercise did not cause the change. The recovered time caused the change, and the exercise was one of the things that filled it.

The specific form does not matter as much as the consistency. Running and lifting and swimming and cycling and sports and yoga and martial arts and walking are all physical activity. The one most likely to stick is the one that does not feel like medicine, the one that has something about it you like, or that puts you in proximity to people you want to see, or that gives you something to measure that you care about. Find the form that works. Then do it in the hours that used to belong to the screen.

The Compounding Effect

Physical fitness and creative output compound in the same way that screen time and sedentary consumption compound, but in the opposite direction. Six months of regular movement produces a body that moves more easily, sleeps better, has more stable energy, and is less dependent on stimulation to feel awake. Six months of screen time produces the opposite: increasing tolerance for stimulation, decreasing ability to tolerate boredom, degraded sleep, accumulated physical stiffness. One path makes the next day easier. The other makes it harder. You are choosing which compound interest you want.

What the First Weeks Actually Feel Like

The honest version of this, because the dishonest version is everywhere: the first two or three weeks of redirecting evening hours from screens to physical activity are uncomfortable in a specific way. The evenings feel longer than they used to. The absence of the screen creates a restlessness that the movement does not immediately fill. You go for the walk and come back and the evening is still there and the phone is still there and the habit is still pulling.

This is normal. It is the nervous system adjusting to a different input level. It passes, usually within two to three weeks of consistent redirection, at which point the walk or the gym session starts to feel like what the screen used to feel like: the thing you do with that slot of time. The difference is that you come back from the physical activity feeling different than when you left. You do not come back from the screen feeling different. You come back feeling like the time passed.

Knowing the adjustment period exists and approximately how long it lasts makes it survivable. Most people quit during the adjustment period because they interpret the discomfort as evidence that the change is not working. It is not evidence of failure. It is evidence of transition.

The Choice

The body does not need a fitness plan or a gym membership or an app that tracks macros. It needs thirty minutes of movement, regularly, in the hours that used to belong to the screen. The specific form is less important than the consistency, and the specific form most likely to produce consistency is the one that does not feel like medicine. The screens will still be there. The body only works for a certain number of years.

The screens will still be there when you get back. The body only works for a certain number of years. Use it while it works.

Chapter 31: Build Real Friendships

Adult Friendship Is Hard. Here Is Why You Have to Do It Anyway.

Adult friendships are one of those things that everyone agrees are important and almost nobody maintains well. Not because people are selfish or lazy, but because the infrastructure that made friendship easy when you were young has disappeared, and the platforms that have moved in to fill the space are doing something that looks like social connection but does not function like it. The conversations chapter earlier in this book covered how to have better interactions with the people in your life. This chapter is about something more specific: the active, deliberate maintenance of close adult friendships that social media has been slowly replacing with a simulation of social connection for the last fifteen years. The difference matters because the simulation does not work, and the loneliness data has been telling us so for decades while we kept scrolling anyway.

Adult friendship is difficult in a way that childhood and adolescent friendship is not. When you are young, proximity creates friendship automatically, you are in the same class, the same neighborhood, the same dorm. You see the same people every day without any effort. The friendships form from the repeated contact.

Adult life removes that automatic proximity. People move. Jobs change. Children arrive and consume the available time. The infrastructure that created friendship without effort disappears, and what remains is friendship by choice. Which requires scheduling, initiative, and the willingness to prioritize it against everything else competing for the same hours. This is genuinely hard. Most people find it harder than it should be and feel vaguely guilty about friendships that have drifted without quite being able to explain why.

What Social Media Did to Friendship

Social media offered what appeared to be a solution to this problem. You could maintain awareness of a large number of people with minimal effort, seeing their updates, liking their posts, commenting occasionally, feeling approximately connected without the friction of actual contact. This felt like having a social life. It was not a social life.

The distinction matters because genuine close friendship, the kind that produces measurable improvements in health, longevity, and psychological wellbeing, requires more than ambient awareness. It requires knowing what someone is going through, being known by them in return, and the experience of having been present for each other through real events over real time. None of that happens through a feed. The feed creates the sensation of connection while substituting for the substance of it.

The result, documented extensively in the loneliness research, is that people have more weak ties, acquaintances and followers and people they vaguely know online, and fewer close friends than previous generations. The number of Americans reporting having no close friends at all has roughly quadrupled since 1990. The U.S. Surgeon General declared loneliness a public health epidemic (Our Epidemic of Loneliness and Isolation, 2023). And yet most people's phones contain multiple apps designed for social connection. The apps are not the problem. The substitution is.

The Mechanics of Maintaining Friendship

Close adult friendship requires three things: regular contact, genuine presence during that contact, and some form of shared experience over time. None of these requires elaborate planning or significant money. They require only that you treat friendship as something that needs tending rather than something that sustains itself automatically.

Regular contact means a specific recurring commitment, not "we should get together soon," which means never, but a standing dinner, a monthly call, a weekly walk, an annual trip that happens because it is on the calendar. The specific format matters less than the regularity. What friendship needs is repeated contact with enough continuity that the relationship builds rather than resets each time.

Genuine presence means the phone is not on the table. It means the conversation is the point, not a background activity while both of you scroll. It means asking follow-up questions about the things someone mentioned last time. It means showing up when something goes wrong, not just when everything is fine and the gathering is easy.

Shared experience over time means doing things together, not just talking about doing things, and not just talking. The meal, the hike, the game, the project, the trip. Experiences create the memories that become the substance of long friendships. Two people who have been through things together, who have the same reference points, who remember the same moments, have something that follows, likes, and comments cannot replicate.

I have a friend I have known for thirty years. For a long stretch in our forties, we went two years with nothing but occasional social media contact, not a falling out, just the drift that happens when proximity disappears and nothing replaces it. What brought it back was a standing monthly dinner, calendared and non-negotiable, started somewhat awkwardly after one of us finally said the obvious thing: we had been meaning to get together for two years and had not. The first dinner felt like catching up with a stranger who shared my entire reference library. The third one felt like no time had passed. The friendship did not require a grand gesture or a significant life event. It required a calendar entry and the willingness to show up to it. That is a low bar. Most drifted friendships clear it easily once someone sets it.

The Traps of Trying

There are specific ways that people fail at maintaining adult friendships, and naming them helps. The first is the planning trap. Two people agree enthusiastically that they should get together, exchange several messages about possible dates, and then the thread dies because coordinating schedules across two busy lives requires someone to pick a date and commit to it. The enthusiasm was real. The follow-through required a specific person to say a specific day and time, and neither person did. This happens so reliably that most adults have multiple friendships stuck permanently in the planning phase, warm in theory and inert in practice.

The second is the reciprocity trap. One person initiates contact repeatedly, the other responds warmly but never initiates. The initiator eventually stops, not out of anger but out of exhaustion, and the friendship drifts because neither person noticed that the maintenance was running in one direction. Social media makes this worse by providing the illusion of mutual contact. You see their posts. They see yours. The monitoring feels like exchange. It is not.

The third is the depth trap. Two people see each other regularly but never move past surface-level conversation. The meals are pleasant. The topics are safe. Neither person has said anything real in months, and the friendship has become a social routine rather than a genuine relationship. This happens more when phones are present, because the phone provides an escape hatch the moment conversation gets uncomfortable, and discomfort is where depth lives.

The fourth, and this one is the most damaging, is the digital maintenance trap. You keep up with someone through likes, comments, birthday messages, and the occasional reaction to a story. You feel connected. You are not connected. You are monitoring. The distinction matters because monitoring produces no shared experience and no actual exchange of information about how either of you is really doing. It produces the feeling of friendship at the cost of the substance of it. When something goes wrong in one of your lives, the monitored friendship has no foundation to support it. The person who liked your posts for three years does not know what to say when you call with real news, because the relationship never developed the capacity for real news.

What Actually Works

The friendships that survive adult life share a few structural features that are not intuitive. They involve a commitment that does not require a decision each time: a standing dinner, a regular call, an annual trip that happens because it is on the calendar, not because both people independently decided this was a good week for it. The decision was made once. The repetition handles the rest.

They involve at least occasional difficulty. The friend who calls when things are hard, not just when things are good. The conversation that includes disagreement, not just validation. The willingness to say something that might not land well because the alternative is a friendship that never goes below the waterline. Difficulty is the mechanism by which friendships deepen. Platforms are designed to eliminate difficulty. That is why platform friendships do not deepen.

They involve doing things together, not just talking. Shared activity creates the memories that become the substance of long friendships. Two people who have cooked together, traveled together, helped each other move, or sat together through something hard have something that no amount of digital contact produces. The activity does not need to be significant. It needs to be shared, in person, with both people present for it.

The Choice

The drift that has accumulated in most adult friendships is not the result of a decision. It is the result of the screen being more immediately available than the phone call, repeatedly, until the gap becomes the default. The book of people who matter is finite. The time to maintain those relationships is not unlimited. The feed will keep generating content long after the people who matter have stopped waiting for someone to reach out.

Chapter 32: Learn a Skill That Takes Years

Why Difficulty Is the Point

Let me describe the specific experience of being bad at something for the first time in a while. It is uncomfortable in a way that the screen has trained you to avoid. Your hands do not cooperate. The gap between what you hear in your head and what comes out is enormous. You want to quit. Your brain suggests that you could be watching something instead. Something good, probably. Something that would not make you feel incompetent. This discomfort is the product.

The skill is on the other side of it. You cannot get to the skill without going through the discomfort, and the algorithm has been very successfully selling you a life in which you never have to feel incompetent at anything because you never try to get good at anything new. Everything covered in this book has been engineered for ease. The swipe is frictionless. The autoplay is smooth. The algorithm knows what you want before you do. The entire architecture of the attention economy is built around reducing the effort required to consume the next piece of content, because effort is the enemy of engagement and engagement is revenue.

This chapter is about the deliberate acquisition of something that cannot be obtained without extended difficulty: a skill that takes years to develop, that requires you to be bad at it for a long time before you are good at it, and that rewards patience in a way that no platform is designed to reward.

The specific skill does not matter. A language. A musical instrument. A martial art. Chess. Woodworking. Coding. A culinary tradition. Sailing. Glassblowing. The common thread is that mastery in these domains takes years of consistent practice, involves extended periods of feeling incompetent, and produces a kind of deep familiarity, with the material, with the process, with your own learning, that quick consumption cannot produce.

What the Algorithm Has Done to Your Patience

The TikTok chapter described how fifteen-second content has compressed the brain's tolerance for delayed gratification. The gaming chapter described how digital achievements deliver rewards calibrated to feel meaningful without requiring genuine accomplishment. Both of these represent the same underlying pattern: the systematic replacement of slow reward with fast reward, at scale, over years, until waiting for anything begins to feel intolerable.

Learning a skill that takes years is the antidote to this specific damage. It is not comfortable. The first six months of learning an instrument are genuinely unpleasant, the sounds are bad, the progress is slow, the gap between what you hear in your head and what comes out of your hands is discouraging. A language does not become functional for a year or more of regular practice. A martial art requires showing up repeatedly to be corrected by people who are better than you. The discomfort is structural. It cannot be skipped.

But what happens during that discomfort is precisely what the algorithm has been preventing. Your brain relearns that effort produces reward, not instantly, not with a variable schedule designed to keep you engaged, but reliably and cumulatively over time. The improvement that comes from a year of practice is not a notification. It is a capacity you now have that you did not have before. It lives in your body or your mind and it does not disappear when you close the app.

What the First Year Actually Looks Like

I want to be specific about what six months of learning something hard feels like, because the motivational framing of skill acquisition usually skips this part. It feels like being wrong, repeatedly, in front of the material. The language student who cannot follow a conversation. The musician who plays the same four bars incorrectly for the third week running. The martial artist who gets corrected on the same technique by the same instructor for the fourth class in a row. The feeling is not one of progress. It is one of exposure, of being someone who does not yet know how to do this thing, in contact with that fact, with no shortcut available.

The algorithm has made this feeling unusual rather than normal. Most of what the algorithm serves you has been filtered for competence: finished products, polished performances, expert demonstrations. You rarely see the first year of anything. This means most people have lost the experiential reference point for what genuine learning feels like. When it arrives, when they pick up the instrument or start the language and encounter the actual gap between where they are and where they want to be, it registers as something being wrong rather than as the normal texture of acquiring something real.

Nothing is wrong. You are in the first year. The first year is supposed to feel like this. Everyone who is now good at the thing you are trying to learn spent a first year that felt exactly like yours does. They continued anyway. That is the entire secret.

The Compounding That Matters

Skills compound in a way that content consumption does not. The person who has spent three years learning a language is not just three years' worth of experience ahead of the person who started yesterday. They are in a qualitatively different relationship with that language. They have the accumulated context of everything they have read, heard, and spoken in it. They have the cognitive infrastructure that allows new input to be processed quickly because it connects to so much that already exists.

The person who has watched ten thousand hours of television has seen a lot of television. They do not have a capacity that someone who watched less television lacks. The time was spent; nothing was built.

Every hour you put into a multi-year skill is an hour that compounds. Every hour you put into passive consumption is an hour that does not. This is not a moral argument. It is arithmetic.

The Choice

You do not need to decide which skill tonight. But you do need to pick one, one specific thing, not "I want to be more creative" or "I should learn something new." Something specific enough that there is a clear first step: a class to sign up for, a teacher to find, a book to buy, an instrument to rent. Something you are willing to be bad at for six months before deciding whether it is for you.

The platforms have trained you to expect competence immediately and to abandon things that do not deliver satisfaction quickly. Learning a skill that takes years is partly an act of reclaiming the longer timeline from the shorter one. It is the investment in a future version of yourself that the algorithm has no interest in helping you build.

Chapter 33: Be Somewhere Without Documenting It

The Camera Has Become the Barrier

There is a photograph you have never taken. It exists in a specific moment in your life when something was beautiful or moving or important and you did not reach for your phone. You were just there for it. You remember it not as an image but as a feeling, the quality of the light, the specific weight of the moment, the way it felt to be in that place at that time without any mediation between you and the experience.

Most people have fewer of these memories than they should, because the reflex to document has colonized the space where presence used to live. The concert where you watched the whole thing through a four-inch screen. The meal that was photographed from three angles before anyone ate. The sunset interrupted by the decision about which filter. The child's first steps recorded on a phone that the child will never watch, held by a parent who was technically there but experientially somewhere else, in the future moment of sharing the video, rather than in the present moment of witnessing the thing.

What Documentation Does to Experience

There is research on this, and it confirms what most people already suspect. The act of photographing an experience for external sharing activates the part of the brain concerned with how the thing will appear to others, which is a different cognitive process from being absorbed in the experience itself. The two states are not compatible in the same moment. You can be documenting or you can be present, and the phone has made documentation so frictionless and so socially rewarded that it has become the default, leaving presence as the thing you have to choose deliberately.

The memory research is equally interesting. People who photograph experiences with the intention of posting them subsequently remember those experiences less clearly than people who did not photograph them. The outsourcing of the memory to the device interferes with the encoding of the memory in the mind. You have the photograph. You do not have the experience. These are not the same thing.

What You Are Actually Missing

Travel is where this is most obvious and most damaging. The Instagram travel chapter earlier in this book covered the illusion of experience through other people's photographs. This chapter is about what you miss in your own experience when the documentation impulse takes over.

A city you visit while constantly photographing it is a set of compositions. A city you visit with your phone in your pocket is a place. The difference is not about the photographs, some photographs are worth taking. It is about the default setting. When the camera is always the first response to anything interesting, you develop a relationship with the surface of your experience rather than its depth. You know what it looked like. You do not always know what it felt like.

The same dynamic applies to meals, concerts, family gatherings, nature, and ordinary moments that are not conventionally photographable but that constitute the actual texture of a life. The habit of documentation, once established, does not spare the undramatic moments. It trains the eye to evaluate every moment for its shareable qualities, which means living in a continuous audition for content rather than in the actual experience of being alive.

I have been to concerts where I kept the phone in my pocket the entire time. I remember those concerts differently from the ones where I filmed. The filmed ones exist as footage I have not opened. The others exist as experiences that are still present. This is not a theory about memory. It is just what happened.

The Social Cost of Not Documenting

Part of what makes the documentation reflex hard to break is that it is socially expected. When you attend an event and do not post about it, people who follow you do not know you were there. When you travel and do not document it, the trip does not enter the social record in the way that documented trips do. There is a real, if diffuse, social pressure built into the sharing economy: the person who posts is present in the feed; the person who does not has, in some algorithmic sense, not been anywhere.

This pressure is worth naming because pretending it does not exist makes it harder to work against. Choosing to be somewhere without documenting it is not a private decision. It is a small act of withdrawal from a social contract that many people around you are still honoring. You will occasionally be asked why you did not post the trip, the concert, the dinner. The honest answer, that you were trying to be there, will seem unusual to some people, which tells you something about how far the default has shifted.

The trade is worth it. The social acknowledgment of having been somewhere is much thinner than the actual experience of having been there. What you are giving up when you put the phone away is other people's confirmation that the experience happened. What you are keeping is the experience. These are not equivalent things, and one of them disappears if you spend the evening documenting it.

The Practice

The practice is simple: leave the phone in your pocket. Or at home. For a defined period, in a defined context. Not forever. Not as a rule. As an experiment, repeated until it becomes a choice rather than a deprivation.

The entry point is a specific context, not a general resolution. One meal per week eaten without photographing it. One event attended with the phone in a pocket or left at home. One trip where the photographs are chosen deliberately rather than reflexively. The purpose is not the reduction in photographs. It is the noticing. What changes in attention and memory when the experience is inhabited rather than framed is the data worth collecting.

The photographs you do not take will not be missed. The experiences you are fully present for will be.

The Choice

The sharing reflex has become so automatic that many people no longer experience the moment before they have already decided how to frame it for an audience. The question "what is this like?" has been replaced by "how does this look?" These are genuinely different orientations to living, and only one of them produces the kind of memories that sustain a person over time. Being somewhere without an intermediary, without the device between you and the thing happening, is not a sacrifice. It is what presence is. The experience existed without anyone's acknowledgment. So did you.

Chapter 34: Build Something Financially Real

The Productive Use of Recovered Hours

The introduction to this book mentioned the number of books I have written. I am not repeating it here as a standard anyone should feel obligated to meet. I am repeating the source: an unplugged television and a decade of evenings that were mine to use. This book has covered what passive consumption costs in time. A thousand hours a year is a conservative estimate of what the average person spends on television, streaming, social media, and digital entertainment combined. This chapter is about what is possible when a meaningful fraction of that time is redirected to economic output as well as personal enrichment.

The mathematics are not complicated. One thousand hours a year is roughly twenty hours per week. Twenty hours per week is the equivalent of a half-time job. People who hold half-time jobs produce half-time output. What would you build with a half-time job's worth of focused effort, directed at something you have been meaning to start for years?

What the Recovered Hours Actually Enable

In 2014, I recovered roughly twenty hours per week from the television and redirected them to writing. In the decade since, that redirection has produced the books, the ghostwriting business, a book coaching practice, a newsletter with tens of thousands of readers, and a body of published work that continues to generate income. None of that output came from unusual talent or exceptional discipline. It came from showing up in the hours that were previously occupied by a screen.

The specific output will be different for different people. A software developer who reclaims evenings could build the side project that becomes a product. A person with domain expertise in any field could write the book that establishes them as a credible authority. A skilled tradesperson could document their knowledge and sell courses. An entrepreneur with a business idea could spend the recovered time on market research, prototyping, or the first customers. The common thread is not the specific activity. It is the application of recovered time to something with accumulating value.

Why This Is Different From "Hustle Culture"

This is not hustle culture. Hustle culture asks you to replace sleep and relationships with work. This book is asking you to replace passive consumption with purposeful activity. Which is a completely different trade. The hours going to television and social media were not rest. For most people they were a default: the thing that happened when nothing else was planned. Replacing a default with a purpose is not grinding.

A practical note on what 'something with accumulating value' looks like across different lives: the nurse who uses recovered evenings to build the health literacy platform she has been thinking about for three years. The tradesperson who starts documenting their process on video and finds an audience among people who want to learn the trade. The teacher who writes the curriculum materials that schools have been paying consultants to produce. The person with thirty years of domain expertise in any field who writes the book that did not exist before they wrote it. The software developer who builds the tool their whole industry wishes existed. The common thread is not talent or capital. It is redirected time applied consistently to something specific.

Starting Small and Staying Consistent

The recovered hours do not all need to go to financial output. Many of them should go to the other chapters in this section: making things for their own sake, moving your body, maintaining friendships, learning skills that take years. A full life is not a maximally productive one.

But some of those hours, even five or ten per week, directed consistently at something with accumulating value will produce results that compound over years. The book that takes two years of weekend mornings to write is still a book. The business that grows slowly from a side project is still a business. The skill that opens a new income stream after three years of practice is still a skill that generates income. The timeline is longer than the algorithm has trained you to expect. The result is more durable than anything the algorithm can offer.

The Permission

There is a version of this conversation that treats financial ambition as something you need to justify. You do not. Wanting to build something that earns money, that creates security, that compounds over years into a body of work or a business or a financial position that is genuinely yours, is not shallow. It is what people have always done with their working hours when they controlled those hours. The culture that tells you ambition is crass while selling you subscriptions you cannot afford has a financial interest in your passivity. The platforms have been spending your hours for you, with your consent, one evening at a time. The scrolling has not made you richer, more secure, or more free. It has made the platform more profitable. That is the trade you have been making, and you can stop making it any time you decide to.

A note for readers whose working years are behind them: the redirect does not require a business plan. The retired teacher who writes the book about teaching that no one else wrote. The grandparent who documents the family history before it disappears. The volunteer who shows up with twenty hours a week of recovered time and a lifetime of skills the organization needs. The person who mentors the younger version of themselves through something they learned the hard way. These are not lesser versions of the redirect. They are the version that comes with the one thing younger readers do not have: enough experience to know exactly what is worth building.

The Choice

The thousand hours are not hypothetical. They exist. They are going somewhere right now. Every one of them. The person who spends those hours on the consuming side of every platform they own arrives at the end of each year with nothing to show for it except a vague sense that the year went fast. The person who redirects even a quarter of those hours, two hundred and fifty hours, five hours a week, toward something with accumulating value arrives at the end of the year with a thing that did not exist before: a manuscript, a business with its first customers, a financial picture that is clear instead of anxious, a skill that opens a door that was closed. The difference between those two years is not talent or luck.

It is where the hours went. And the hours go where the defaults send them, unless you change the defaults.

Decide what you are building. Start this week. Use the hours. And if what you are building requires getting the financial infrastructure under control first, understanding the numbers, automating the admin, using the tools that have been sitting unused, Chapter 35 is the map for that.

Chapter 35: Use Technology, Don't Be Used By It

The thousand hours and what to do with them

The diagnosis section of this book made a specific argument about time. The average person spends roughly a thousand hours a year on passive digital consumption, scrolling, streaming, refreshing, watching. This is not an estimate designed to shock. It is arithmetic applied to the numbers that platforms themselves report about daily usage. A thousand hours a year is twenty hours a week. It is, as this book noted early on, the equivalent of a half-time job.

The question this chapter answers is: a half-time job doing what, exactly?

The previous chapters in this section have described redirecting those hours into physical activity, relationships, creative work, and community. All of that is real and valuable. But there is a category this book would be dishonest to ignore: using technology itself, deliberately and productively, to handle the things that currently drain your time, your money, your mental energy, and your sense of control over your own life.

Most people are passive consumers of technology. The contributing side is not only making content for an audience. It is using the tools, AI, spreadsheets, automation, data, to run your life better. The person who spends two hours a week on their finances instead of two hours scrolling is on the contributing side of technology. So is the gig worker who uses AI to handle their invoicing and quarterly taxes. So is the caregiver who uses AI to research a parent's diagnosis and walk into a doctor's appointment with the right questions. So is anyone who uses a tool on purpose to produce a real outcome, rather than being used by a platform that is producing an outcome for someone else. One clarification worth making: contributing to someone else's platform is not the same thing as contributing to your own.

The social media manager, the content moderator, the gig worker building someone else's app, these people are on the contributing side of technology but producing for someone else's infrastructure. That is real work. What this book is arguing for, in addition, is using some of the recovered hours to build something that accumulates value for you.

The admin that is eating your evenings

Here is a specific number: the average self-employed person in the United States spends between five and seven hours per week on administrative tasks, scheduling, invoicing, bookkeeping, client communication, estimates, follow-up. That is time they are not working, not resting, and not living. It is the overhead cost of running a small operation without the systems that larger organizations take for granted.

AI tools have largely eliminated the difficulty of most of these tasks. A plumber who describes a job and asks AI to generate a professional invoice is not doing something exotic. A freelance designer who uses AI to draft a client proposal from bullet points is not cheating. A bookkeeper who uses a spreadsheet template and AI to categorize transactions before handing them to an accountant has compressed three hours of Sunday anxiety into twenty minutes of Tuesday efficiency. These are not futuristic scenarios. They are available right now, free or nearly free, to anyone with a phone and a few hours to learn how to use them.

The scrolling hours are the exact hours this work has been competing against. The reason most people's admin pile up is not that they lack the ability to address it. It is that the phone is right there, always more immediately rewarding than a tax form, and the pile grows until it becomes a crisis. Redirecting even a fraction of the passive consumption hours toward the admin that currently runs you, rather than you running it, is one of the most direct improvements available.

I spend about twenty minutes a week on my own finances now. A spreadsheet, a few categories, the numbers from the previous week. I put this off for years because the pile felt large. It was not large. The pile felt large because I had trained myself to scroll past it the same way I scrolled past everything else that required sitting still with something uncomfortable. The scrolling did not make the pile smaller. It just made it easier to not look at.

Knowing your money

Financial illiteracy is not a character flaw. It is the predictable result of a financial system designed to be opaque, combined with a digital environment designed to make spending frictionless and invisible. Most people have no reliable sense of where their money goes. They know their income. They know when the account runs low. Everything in between is a fog that occasionally produces unpleasant surprises.

A spreadsheet solves this. Not a budgeting app with a subscription fee and a gamified interface, a spreadsheet, which is free, permanent, yours, and which requires you to look at the numbers rather than having an algorithm summarize them into a score. The person who spends ninety minutes one Sunday building a simple income-and-expense tracker, and then spends twenty minutes each week maintaining it, knows more about their financial life than most people who earn twice as much. That knowledge compounds. It changes decisions. It reveals where the money is going, which is almost always different from where people think it is going.

AI makes this more accessible than it has ever been. You can describe your situation to an AI tool and ask it to help you build the spreadsheet. You can paste in a list of transactions and ask it to categorize them. You can ask it to explain what a tax form is asking for in plain language. You can use it to check whether a financial decision makes mathematical sense before you make it. These are not activities that require financial expertise. They require only the willingness to spend the time that currently goes to scrolling on something that will still matter next year.

AI as a research and decision tool

One of the most valuable uses of AI tools is one that the content creation conversation almost entirely obscures: using AI to help you make better decisions about your actual life.

The caregiver whose parent has been diagnosed with something serious and who needs to understand treatment options, ask the right questions at appointments, and deal with a medical system that assumes you already know how it works, that person can use AI to compress weeks of confusing research into hours of useful preparation. The person buying a used car who wants to understand what questions to ask, what to look for in an inspection, and what a fair price looks like, that person can use AI to walk into the negotiation informed rather than exposed. The person considering a career change who wants to understand what skills are required, what the job market looks like, and what the transition path might realistically involve, that person can use AI to get honest, specific information that previously required either expensive professional advice or years of trial and error.

This is AI on the contributing side: you arrive with a real problem, a genuine question, or a decision that matters, and you use the tool to think through it more carefully than you could alone. The output is not content. The output is a better decision, a more informed conversation, a clearer understanding of something that was previously opaque. This is also where the author test from Chapter 2 applies cleanly. You are the author of the decision. The tool helped you think. That is the right relationship.

Automation and the recovery of your time

Beyond AI specifically, the broader category of digital automation has made it possible to eliminate entire classes of recurring tasks that previously required sustained human attention. Automatic savings transfers mean money moves to where you decided it should go without requiring you to remember to do it. Subscription management tools surface the recurring charges you forgot you were paying for. Calendar systems handle scheduling coordination that used to require back-and-forth email chains. Password managers eliminate the cognitive overhead of managing credentials across dozens of services. Bill payment automation eliminates late fees from forgetting.

None of these are dramatic. They are maintenance, the category of task that is not difficult but that must be done repeatedly, and that accumulates into a significant ongoing time cost if handled manually. Setting up these systems takes an afternoon. The payoff is measured in years. The afternoon you spend automating your savings transfer is the last afternoon you will ever have to spend thinking about whether you remembered to do it.

The relevant comparison is not 'automation versus doing the task manually.' It is 'the afternoon setting up automation versus the hours per year of scrolling that currently fill the time those recurring tasks don't quite get.' The scrolling does not handle the admin. The scrolling just makes the admin feel more distant and more daunting until it becomes a crisis.

Content creation is one option among many

This chapter has covered practical financial control, administrative automation, AI-assisted decision-making, and the recovery of time from tasks that currently run you. Content creation belongs on this list, building an audience for work you are doing, teaching what you know, using platforms as distribution for genuine expertise, but it is one option, not the model.

The people who benefit most from the argument of this book are not necessarily people who want to become creators. They are people who are currently spending a thousand hours a year on passive consumption and getting nothing back for it, not rest, not pleasure, not growth, not financial security, not better decisions, not recovered time. The redirect can go anywhere. What matters is that it goes somewhere you chose, toward something that compounds in your favor.

A freelancer whose invoicing now takes twenty minutes instead of two hours has redirected time. A parent who understands their family's finances instead of being vaguely anxious about them has redirected attention. A person who walked into a difficult medical conversation prepared instead of overwhelmed has redirected AI from passive tool to genuine support. A household that runs on a few well-chosen automated systems instead of recurring manual effort has redirected cognitive load.

None of these require an audience. None of them require a camera. All of them require the same thing: the decision to use the tool rather than be used by it.

You do not own the platform

One caution applies to every digital strategy in this chapter, and it applies whether you are building an audience, running a business, or managing your finances: do not build your entire operation on infrastructure you do not control.

Your primary home online should be something you own, a domain you registered, hosted by a service you pay for directly. Your financial records should live somewhere you control, not only inside an app that can change its terms or shut down. Your email list, if you build one, is yours in a way that social media followers are not. Your spreadsheets and documents, backed up somewhere you own, survive any platform collapse. The platforms are useful. They are also rented land. Build on owned ground first, distribute to rented platforms second.

Where the scrolling hours go

The honest version of this chapter's argument is simple. You already have the time. You have been spending it on platforms designed to take it from you and give you very little in return. The redirect is not asking you to become a different person or develop skills you do not have. It is asking you to point the same hours at things that work for you rather than for the platform.

Twenty minutes a week on a spreadsheet versus twenty minutes of scrolling. The scrolling leaves nothing. The spreadsheet leaves you knowing where you stand.

An hour with an AI tool preparing for a difficult conversation versus an hour doomscrolling before it. The scrolling leaves you more anxious. The preparation leaves you more capable.

A Sunday afternoon setting up automation for the admin that has been piling up versus a Sunday afternoon on Netflix with the admin still waiting. The Netflix leaves the pile. The automation makes the pile smaller every week for the rest of your life.

The thousand hours are not a gift waiting to be claimed. They are already being spent. The question is whether they are being spent for you or for the platform. That is the only question this chapter is asking. The answer is entirely up to you.

The choice

You do not have to become a creator. You do not have to build an audience or start a business or produce anything for anyone else to consume. You have to decide that the hours going to passive consumption should go somewhere that matters to you instead, and then pick the one or two things from this chapter that would make the biggest difference in your actual life.

The tools are there. The time is there. The only thing missing is the decision to use one in place of the other.

Start with one thing. The simplest thing on the list. The thing that would make the most obvious difference if you did it. Do that before you touch the phone tomorrow night.

The feed will still be there when you are done. But so will whatever you built.

Chapter 36: Find Your Community

What Institutions Give You That a Feed Cannot

The friendships chapter covered one-to-one relationships. This chapter is about something different: the larger structures of shared life that have been quietly hollowing out as screens have filled the hours that community used to occupy. And yes, I know what "community" sounds like. It sounds like something a wellness influencer says while holding a latte. Bear with me, because the data on what the collapse of community participation has done to people is genuinely alarming, and the solution is considerably more practical than it sounds.

There is a specific version of this problem that the rest of this book has not fully named: the person who is not on their phone out of habit or addiction, but out of loneliness. The retired person whose children live far away. The recently bereaved. The person who moved to a new city and has not yet built the social infrastructure that makes an evening without a screen feel like a choice rather than an absence. For these readers, the screen is not a substitute for a better use of time. It is a substitute for company. The argument this book makes about passive consumption applies, but the solution is not a redirect toward productivity. It is a redirect toward presence, toward the institutions and structures that put you in a room with other people repeatedly, over time, until the room starts to feel like somewhere you belong. That is what this chapter is about, and it is addressed directly to you.

A community is not a group of people who follow the same account. It is a group of people who show up in the same place, repeatedly, over time, with some shared purpose that requires their physical presence. Religious congregations, civic organizations, sports leagues, volunteer groups, neighborhood associations, unions, service clubs, professional guilds, bands, choirs, community theater, maker spaces, running clubs, martial arts studios, all of these are communities in the structural sense. They have regular meetings. They have rituals. They have roles and responsibilities. They remember when you are absent. They change when you are present.

Membership in these kinds of institutions has declined substantially in most Western countries over the past fifty years, and the decline has accelerated in the smartphone era. The sociologist Robert Putnam documented the collapse of American civic participation in his 2000 book Bowling Alone, noting the decline of everything from bowling leagues to PTA membership to church attendance to voter turnout. He wrote it before social media existed. The trends he identified have continued and deepened since.

What Community Does That Friendship Alone Cannot

The distinction between friendship and community matters. A close friend is irreplaceable. But a community provides things that even close friendships do not: a context that is larger than any individual relationship, a sense of continuity across time, roles and responsibilities that make you accountable to people beyond your immediate circle, and the experience of working toward something that matters beyond your own life.

The research on community participation and wellbeing is consistent. People who are embedded in functioning communities, who attend regularly, who have roles, who are known, report higher levels of meaning and life satisfaction than people who have equivalent numbers of individual friendships but no community membership. The mechanism appears to be partly the sense of belonging to something larger than oneself, and partly the regular reminder that there are people whose lives are different from yours, with different problems and different resources, whose wellbeing is partly your responsibility and whose presence enriches yours.

The screen has been a very effective substitute for the feeling of community without the substance of it. The online group, the Discord server, the Facebook group, the comment section where the same people appear regularly, these produce the social recognition and the sense of shared identity that community provides, without the physical co-presence, the accountability, the shared work, or the genuine interdependence. They are community-flavored products. The actual nutrition is missing.

The Barrier Is Showing Up

The main reason people are not embedded in communities is not that communities do not exist. They exist everywhere. There is a congregation, a running club, a woodworking guild, a volunteer organization, or a rec sports league within driving distance of almost every person reading this book. The reason people are not in them is simpler and less flattering: the friction of joining and attending feels higher than the friction of staying home with the phone. The first few times you go anywhere new, a congregation, a club meeting, a volunteer orientation, a sports league tryout, it is awkward. You do not know anyone. The rhythms are unfamiliar. The established members have relationships with each other that you do not yet share. It takes several visits before you feel like you belong, and several more before you do.

The screen removes that awkwardness by being always available, already familiar, and never socially risky. Choosing the screen over the community meeting is not laziness. It is a rational response to the relative friction of each option, in a context where one has been engineered to be maximally frictionless. The fix is not to berate yourself for taking the easy path. It is to recognize that the awkward path leads somewhere the easy one does not, and to choose the awkward path deliberately a few times until it becomes familiar.

I am not naturally social in large groups. I find the first visit to anything new uncomfortable in the specific way this chapter describes: the unfamiliar rhythms, the established relationships I am not part of yet, the uncertainty about whether I belong. I have shown up to things I did not want to show up to and been glad I went. The awkwardness is temporary. I have never once been glad I stayed home instead.

Finding the Right One

The community that will work for you is the one organized around something you already care about, or something you want to learn, in a form that requires physical attendance. Religious community if you have religious inclinations. A sport if you are physically inclined. A creative pursuit if that is your direction. A service organization if contribution to something practical motivates you. The specific vehicle matters less than whether you would be willing to show up for it when you do not feel like it. That willingness is the test.

Attend three times before you evaluate. The first time is orientation. The second time is the beginning of recognition. The third time is when you start to have a sense of whether this is a place where you could belong. Most people leave after the first awkward visit and conclude the community is not for them. They have not given it enough time to become familiar, and familiar is what community requires before it becomes sustaining.

The Choice

The community worth joining is already there. The loneliness epidemic and the collapse of civic participation are not individual failures. They are the downstream consequences of an economy that profits from isolation and an entertainment infrastructure that has made staying home with a screen the path of least resistance. What counteracts both is the same thing it has always been: a room with other people in it, a shared purpose, and enough repeated contact for familiarity to develop. The awkwardness is temporary. The belonging, if you stay, is cumulative. The people who will be glad you showed up are already in the room. They are just waiting for you to walk through the door.

Chapter 37: What Intentional Looks Like

The Honest Version of a Digital Life That Works

The honest version of what this book describes looks like this: I use digital tools from the moment I wake up until the moment I go to sleep.

I check messages in the morning. I write on a computer. I use AI tools for research and editing. I communicate with clients through platforms. I manage my business through software. I look things up constantly. I am, by any objective measure, a heavy technology user. I have been one for decades, and I expect to remain one.

So when I tell you to turn off the TV and get off your ass, I am not describing a life without screens. I am describing a life where the screens you use are working for you rather than the other way around. That distinction is the entire point of this book, and this chapter is where I lay it out plainly.

The Line That Matters

There is a line in digital life that most people have never consciously drawn. On one side: tools you use to produce something. On the other: platforms that use you to produce something for them.

When I write a book on my computer, the computer is serving me. When I research a topic online to complete a client project, the internet is serving me. When I use AI to edit a draft I have already written, the tool is serving me. In each case, I had a goal before I opened the application, and the application helped me reach it. I closed the application when the task was done.

When I scroll through social media with no specific purpose, the platform is using me. When I binge-watch a show because the next episode autostarted and stopping feels like friction, the platform is using me. When I check my phone every few minutes not because I expect anything important but because the habit has its own momentum, the device is using me. In each case, the platform had a goal, to capture my attention and convert it into engagement metrics, and I was serving it.

This is the line. It is not about screen time totals. It is about who is in control of the session.

What I Keep

I keep every tool that helps me produce work: writing software, research tools, communication platforms for client work, AI tools used deliberately for specific tasks. I keep the phone because I use it to call people and manage my business. I keep email because I have a business that requires it, managed at scheduled times rather than continuously. I keep a small number of websites I read on purpose, when I decide to read them.

What I do not keep: social media platforms whose business model depends on maximizing the time I spend on them. Streaming services running continuously in the background. News sources designed to generate emotional reactions rather than inform. Apps whose primary function is to give me something to do with my hands when I am bored.

The dividing line I use: does this tool make me more capable, or does it make me more dependent? Does using it leave me with something, a finished piece of work, useful information, a completed task, or does it leave me with a vague sense of having been somewhere online for a while?

The Productivity That Actually Happened

Here is what the last decade of deliberate digital use has produced: the books you have heard about by now. A successful ghostwriting and book coaching business. Dozens of author clients helped to complete and publish their own books. Interviews, articles, a newsletter with tens of thousands of subscribers. All of this was done with heavy technology use, every day, for years.

The difference between this and a decade of heavy passive consumption is not the number of hours in front of a screen. It is what happened during those hours. The screens were pointed at production rather than consumption. The tools were chosen for what they enabled rather than for what they provided. The sessions had beginnings and ends determined by me rather than by an algorithm optimized to keep me engaged.

This is what deliberate digital use looks like. It is not a monk's phone. It is not a minimalist device with three apps. It is a full-featured, heavily used digital life where you are the one deciding what the screens are for.

The Practical Map

If you want a concrete model, here is how the deliberate digital day works. Morning: work tools only. Writing, client communications, research for active projects. No social media, no news, no browsing. The first hours of the day are the most cognitively productive; they should not be spent giving attention to platforms that want it.

Midday: a break that is an actual break. Not checking your phone while eating. Not scrolling while walking. Eating, walking, talking to a person, or doing nothing. Something that is different from the work session rather than a continuation of the screen session in a different register.

Afternoon: more work. Work messaging checked at defined times rather than continuously. The focus protection that was in place in the morning continues.

Evening: genuine personal time. This is the slot that the old television habit occupied. What fills it now, reading, exercise, conversation, a hobby, twenty minutes on the finances you have been meaning to look at, a side project, an admin task you will complete, matters less than the reality that it is not filling itself automatically with content chosen by an algorithm. Occasional deliberate entertainment is fine. A show you chose to watch, watched on purpose, turned off when it ends. That is different from the television that runs because stopping requires a decision.

This is not a rigid schedule. It is a set of defaults. The default in the morning is work, not browsing. The default in the evening is chosen activity, not passive consumption. The default when bored is something real, not a phone. Defaults shape behavior more reliably than willpower does, and changing your defaults is the practical work of everything in this book.

The Permission

You have permission to use technology heavily. You have permission to build a career on it, to be online most of the day, to use every tool that makes you more capable and more productive. None of that is the problem this book is about.

The problem this book is about is the specific category of digital activity that produces nothing, serves no purpose you chose, and exists primarily because someone else profits from keeping you engaged. The television that runs by default. The feed you scroll because stopping is harder than continuing. The notification you respond to because not responding creates anxiety. The platform that has trained you to be its product rather than its user.

Cut that. Keep everything else. The line between them is clearer than it first appears, and once you see it, you cannot unsee it.

The Choice

You do not have to choose between technology and life. That is a false binary that makes the whole project seem more extreme than it is. You have to choose between technology that serves your life and technology that substitutes for it. Between digital activity that produces something and digital activity that merely consumes time.

The tools are not the enemy. The defaults are. Change the defaults, and the tools become what they were always supposed to be: instruments of your intentions, not replacements for them.

Chapter 38: A Year Later

What Sticks, What Doesn't, and What You Actually Build

A year after unplugging the television, the cable box is still in the closet. I know because I have never had reason to open that closet for anything else. That is not a metaphor. That is a physical fact about a piece of hardware that has been in a closet for over a decade, untouched, because nothing about my life has required it.

This chapter is about what happens after the thirty days. Not the dramatic transformation version, the one where you emerge from a month of digital restraint as a completely different person who runs marathons and reads Tolstoy. That version is mostly marketing. The real version is quieter and more useful: certain things stick, certain things require ongoing maintenance, certain things you discover you did not miss, and certain things you rebuild from scratch in ways you did not expect.

What Sticks Without Effort

The habits that require no maintenance after the first thirty days are the ones where the old behavior is no longer available. If you cancelled the streaming service, you cannot absent-mindedly binge it. If you deleted the social media app, you cannot compulsively check it. Removal is the most reliable form of change because it eliminates the decision entirely. You do not have to be disciplined about something that is not there.

The habits that also tend to stick with minimal effort: morning routines that do not start with screens, because the brain learns quickly that the day begins differently now. Regular physical movement, once the body has had a few weeks to remember it prefers it. Reading before bed instead of scrolling, once the book is on the nightstand and the phone is across the room. These become defaults faster than people expect, because habits are largely environmental. Change the environment and the habit often changes with it.

What Requires Ongoing Vigilance

Some things do not become automatic. Work messaging is one of them, the pull of the inbox reasserts itself whenever work gets stressful, because checking feels like doing something about the stress even when it is not. Social media has a way of creeping back in through side doors: a platform you kept for professional reasons that gradually starts functioning as a personal one, a news source that turns into a scroll habit, a YouTube search for something specific that turns into forty minutes of related videos.

The vigilance required is not dramatic. It is a periodic audit, every few months, look at what has crept back in. Not with guilt or self-judgment, but with the same practical question: is this serving me, or am I serving it? If the answer has shifted, remove it again. The thirty-day plan is not a one-time event. It is a template you return to when the drift has accumulated enough to matter.

What You Discover You Did Not Miss

This is the part nobody tells you because it sounds too good to be true, but it is consistently reported by people who make these changes: within a few months, you stop missing most of what you gave up. Not because you have achieved enlightenment, but because the absence has revealed the thing for what it was, a habit, not a need.

You do not miss the television you got rid of. You miss the comfort of having something to do at the end of the day that requires nothing of you, and that need gets met by something else. You do not miss the social media platform you deleted. You miss the social connection it provided the illusion of, and that need gets met, if you let it, by actual contact with actual people. The platform was never really what you wanted. It was a low-friction substitute for something harder and better.

The news you stopped following: you will find out about genuinely important things anyway, and your quality of life will improve measurably from not starting every morning with a list of things to be afraid of. This surprises people more than anything else. The anxiety they attributed to the world was partly the anxiety of consuming news designed to generate anxiety. Remove the source and some of the anxiety goes with it.

What You Build Instead

The most important thing that happens in the year after the thirty days is not what you remove. It is what you build in the space that opens up. This is where the variation between people becomes interesting, because what fills the screen-shaped hole is different for everyone, and discovering what fills it for you is one of the more genuinely interesting things the process produces.

For me it was writing. That was always there, waiting for the hours to become available. For others it has been physical fitness that finally took hold because there was time for it. Relationships that deepened because phones stopped competing for attention during meals. Creative projects that had been "on hold" for years suddenly unblocked by available evenings. Skills acquired, places visited, communities joined. The common thread is not the specific activity. It is the quality of engagement. Things chosen, pursued deliberately, completed. The opposite of passive consumption.

What surprised me most about the year after unplugging was not the productivity. It was how the quality of attention changed. The first few weeks felt restless, the brain reaching for the absent feed the way a tongue finds a missing tooth. By month three, the restlessness had been replaced by something I did not expect: boredom. Not the anxious boredom of a phone you are not checking. The quieter kind, where nothing is happening and your brain starts producing things on its own. Ideas you did not sit down to have start arriving. You notice connections between things you read months apart. You find the opening paragraph of something you had not known you wanted to write. Boredom is the raw material the creative process runs on. The feed had been consuming it before it could accumulate.

By month six, the default had shifted far enough that the old behavior felt foreign. I visited someone who had the television running as background noise and found the sound physically distracting in a way it never had been before. Not because I had become a monk. Because my nervous system had recalibrated to a lower baseline of stimulation, and the constant noise and movement of the screen registered as intrusive rather than normal. This recalibration is not unique to me. People who make these changes report the same thing: the old defaults start to feel like what they are, which is loud.

By month twelve, the question had flipped. It was no longer why I had stopped watching television. It was how I had ever found the time. The hours that had seemed to belong to the screen had been absorbed so completely by writing, reading, walking, cooking, and talking to the people in my life that retrieving them for passive consumption would have required giving up things I now valued. The screen had never been filling empty time. It had been displacing full time. I just could not see what it was displacing until it stopped.

You will not know what yours is until you make the space. That is the point of the space.

The Choice

The story does not end at thirty days. It starts there. The thirty days break the automatic nature of the old habits and give you enough distance to see them clearly. What you do with that distance is the actual work, and it is work that continues, not a project you complete and file away.

A year from now, your relationship with technology will look different from how it looks today. The only question is whether it will look different because you decided how it should look, or because the platforms decided for you. They have been working on their version since you got your first smartphone. You have just started working on yours.

Keep going.

Chapter 39: Your First Thirty Days

A Practical Plan for People Who Hate Practical Plans

Here is the problem with most digital detox advice: it tells you what to stop doing without telling you what to do instead. "Use your phone less" is not a plan. "Spend more time in nature" is not a plan. "Be more present" is the kind of advice that sounds profound at 11 PM while scrolling through Instagram and means absolutely nothing at 7 PM on a Tuesday when you're bored and the remote is right there.

What follows is a thirty-day plan. It is organized by week because attempting everything at once is how people fail at this, abandon the whole project, and end up binge-watching television to recover from the stress of trying to watch less television. One week at a time. Each week adds to the previous one. By day thirty, you will have built a different set of default habits, not through willpower, but through repetition until the new behavior requires less effort than the old one.

A few ground rules before we start. First: this is not a competition. There is no prize for radical transformation and no punishment for imperfect execution. Second: you will slip. You will pick up your phone out of habit, watch one more episode than you intended, and fall asleep with the TV on. This is not failure. This is Tuesday. Note it, move on, try again Wednesday. Third: the goal is not to become someone who never watches TV or uses social media. The goal is to become someone who chooses when to do those things instead of defaulting to them whenever nothing else is actively competing for your attention.

This is a redirect, not a detox

A detox removes something. A redirect points something elsewhere. This plan is a redirect. The goal is not to end up with an emptier life, fewer screens, more staring at walls, evenings where nothing happens. The goal is to end up with a fuller one, where the hours that were going to passive consumption are now going to something you are building.

Before you start the audit, decide what you are redirecting toward. Not vaguely, specifically. One thing that has been waiting for the hours. The financial clarity you have been meaning to get. The admin system that would stop the pile from growing. The skill you have been putting off learning. The health habit you keep postponing. The community you have been meaning to join. The project you have been meaning to start. Write it down somewhere physical. The thirty days are not just about reducing what is on the consuming side of the ledger. They are about building what is on the contributing side.

Every time this plan asks you to stop doing something, there is an implicit question: what goes in that space instead? The answer is not 'nothing.' The answer is the thing you wrote down. Each week adds to the reduction. Each week should also add to the build. By day thirty you should have less screen time and more of whatever you decided to create. That is the measure of success.

Week One: The Audit (Days 1–7)

You cannot change habits you cannot see. Week one is not about reducing anything; it is about finding out what is happening.

Day 1: Turn on your phone's built-in screen time tracker and look at last week's numbers. Most people are shocked by what they find. Write the total down somewhere physical, a notepad, a sticky note, the back of an envelope. You want this number in the physical world, not on another screen.

Day 2: Note the three apps consuming the most time. No judgment yet. Just look.

Days 3–5: For three days, every time you pick up your phone, pause for two seconds and ask yourself why. Not rhetorically. Answer it: boredom, habit, anxiety, a specific task? Write the answers down if that helps. The goal is to discover how many times you pick up the phone for no reason you can articulate.

Days 6–7: Audit your subscriptions. Open your bank statement or email and find every recurring charge for streaming, apps, or digital services. Write them down with their monthly cost. Add them up. Most people find a number they were not expecting.

By the end of week one you have a clear picture of the current situation. You have not changed anything. You have just turned the lights on.

Additional audit items this edition adds to the original plan: check your work email and messaging apps, note how many times per day you check them outside working hours. If you have a sports betting account, look at how many sessions you logged this week and your net balance over the past 30 days. If you use AI tools, note whether you reach for them before or after you have thought through the problem yourself. If you wear a fitness tracker, notice whether checking it is informing your decisions or creating anxiety. Write all of this down alongside your screen time numbers. The picture you are building is not just of your entertainment consumption. It is of every digital system that has a claim on your attention.

Week Two: The First Cuts (Days 8–14)

Now you make one change in each of three areas: your phone, your subscriptions, and your evenings. Just one per area. The instinct is to do everything at once; resist it.

Phone: Turn off all non-essential notifications. Keep calls and texts if you want. Turn off every social media app, every news app, every game. The only notifications that should make your phone buzz are ones from actual people who specifically want to reach you. Everything else is a company pulling your attention toward their product. You did not give them permission to do that. Take it back.

Subscriptions: Cancel the streaming service you use least. If you cannot identify which one that is, that is your answer, cancel the one you had to think hardest about. It will probably still be available next month if you want it back. You can always re-subscribe. You cannot re-subscribe to the hours you spent paying for something you did not use.

Evenings: Pick one night this week, just one, where you do not turn on any screen after 7 PM. Make it a weeknight. Plan something specific to fill the time, because "I won't watch TV" is not a plan. Read something. Cook something. Call someone you haven't spoken to in a while. Go for a walk. Have a bath. The activity does not need to be impressive. It needs to be real.

At the end of week two, you will have one fewer subscription, a quieter phone, and one evening in the last seven where you were completely present. That is real progress. It will not feel dramatic. It is not supposed to.

If your audit revealed a work messaging problem: this week, set your email and Slack to check at three scheduled times only, morning, midday, and late afternoon. Remove both apps from your phone's home screen. Turn off all work message notifications outside those windows. You are not quitting your job. You are establishing that the inbox is a tool you check, not a feed that monitors you. If your audit revealed a sports betting habit that concerns you: delete the betting apps from your phone this week. You can reinstall them later if you decide to. The point is to introduce friction where the app has engineered frictionlessness. Distance and delay are the first interventions.

The biggest mistake people make when reducing screen time is treating it as a subtraction problem. They remove the television and stare at the wall. They delete social media and find themselves picking up the phone anyway, checking nothing in particular. Reduction only works if replacement happens at the same time. Week three is about putting something in the space you created.

This is the week I remember most clearly from my own transition. Not because it was difficult, it was not, particularly, but because it was the first week where the evenings felt like mine rather than like a waiting room. The book on the nightstand. The walk I had been postponing for months. The project I had been meaning to start since I could not remember when. None of it was dramatic. All of it was real.

Day 15: Buy a physical book or find one you own and have not read. Put it somewhere you can see it from your couch. Not on a shelf. In front of you. The barrier to picking it up should be lower than the barrier to opening an app.

Day 16: Identify one thing you have been meaning to learn or do, a skill, a project, a hobby, that you have been putting off because you never have time. You now have time. You have been donating it to streaming platforms. Get the materials, make the first call, sign up for the class, or set up the workspace. Not someday. This week.

Days 17–19: Add a daily walk. Twenty minutes minimum. No headphones for the first week, the point is to be present in your physical environment, not to consume a podcast while technically moving your body. You can add music later. Right now, the goal is to be in your body and your neighborhood without anything competing for your attention.

Days 20–21: Expand your intentional evenings from one night per week to two. Same rule: plan what you will do before the evening starts. The enemy of intentional evenings is not temptation. It is the moment at 8 PM when you have no plan and the remote is within reach.

By the end of week three, you should be reading a little, moving daily, and spending two evenings per week without a screen in your hand. The activities filling those evenings do not matter much. The habit of filling them on purpose does.

Week Four: Consolidation (Days 22–30)

Week four is where the changes become yours rather than borrowed from a book. You have three weeks of data now. You know which changes felt easy and which felt like deprivation. You know which replacements stuck and which ones you abandoned. Use that information.

Day 22: Look at your screen time numbers again. Compare them to day one. Most people see a meaningful reduction without having felt dramatically deprived. The hours did not disappear. They moved somewhere else.

Days 23–25: Delete or disable the social media app that costs you the most time and gives you the least in return. Not all of them, unless you want to. Just the worst one. The one that leaves you feeling worse after you use it than before. You know which one it is. You have known for a while.

Days 26–28: Have one real conversation this week that would previously have been a text exchange. Call someone instead of messaging them. Go to the meeting in person instead of joining by video. Knock on your neighbor's door instead of sending an email. One interaction, conducted at human speed, with the full social information, tone, expression, body language, that digital communication removes.

Days 29–30: Do the 48-hour redirect that opens the next chapter. Friday evening to Sunday evening: phone off, laptop closed, no streaming. Use the preparation you have now done over three weeks. You have a book. You have a walk. You have a project. You have, probably, at least one person you should be spending more time with. This is your test run for the kind of weekend that exists in the chapter after this one.

After Day Thirty

The thirty days are not the destination. They are the on-ramp. By day thirty, you will have established a daily walk, two or more intentional evenings per week, at least one fewer streaming subscription, significantly quieter notifications, and a social media diet that you chose rather than one that was chosen for you by an algorithm.

More importantly, you will have proved something to yourself: that the discomfort of changing these habits is temporary, that the world does not end when you miss a notification, and that the time you recover from screens does not feel empty, it feels like yours.

What you do with it from here is your choice. The point of these thirty days was never to hand you a perfect system. It was to remind you that you have one, that you are capable of deciding how your time is spent rather than discovering at 11 PM that it has been spent for you.

What you build in those thirty days, even if it is small, even if it is rough, even if only a handful of people ever see it, is proof that you are on the contributing side of the line. That is the only destination this plan is trying to reach.

Now turn the page. The last chapter covers where all of this goes from here.

Chapter 40: Escape from the Matrix (No, Really)

A step-by-step guide to crossing the line

Congratulations. You have made it through thirty-nine chapters. You know how the platforms work, what they are designed to do to your attention, and why the consuming side of every tool you own is so much easier than the contributing side. The question the rest of the book has been building toward is the only one that matters: now what?

This chapter is not about turning off your devices. It is not about disconnecting from the internet, going screen-free, or remembering what life was like before Wi-Fi. That framing gets it backwards. The tools are not the problem. Your relationship to them is. And relationships can be changed without throwing anything away.

What follows is a practical ten-step sequence for moving from the consuming side to the contributing side, in whatever form that takes for your life. Not a detox. A redirect. The same screens, pointed differently.

Step 1: The 48-hour redirect

Before you can build new habits, you need to break the old defaults long enough to see them clearly. This means taking a temporary break from the digital activities that are consuming your time and attention, not forever, not as a statement, but as an experiment that lasts one weekend.

From Friday evening until Sunday evening, set passive consumption aside. No feeds, no streaming, no browsing. Keep the tools you need, calls, messages, anything work-related if necessary, but close every platform whose primary function is to hold your attention rather than serve your purpose.

This will feel uncomfortable. You will reach for your phone out of habit repeatedly. That reflex is the whole point. Noticing how often you reach for the passive side is the first step toward choosing the contributing side instead.

Use this weekend to notice the gap between where your time is currently going and where you want it to go. That gap is what the rest of these steps are designed to close.

Step 2: Identify your redirect

The 48 hours are not an end in themselves. They are a pause that creates space for a question: what do I want to do with these hours?

This is the question the algorithm never lets you ask, because the algorithm already has an answer and it involves you staying exactly where you are. The pause removes the algorithm's answer long enough for you to form your own.

Be specific. Not 'be more productive' or 'use my phone less.' Something concrete: the financial picture you keep meaning to get clear on; the skill you have been meaning to develop; the project waiting for the hours; the admin system that would get the pile under control; the physical practice you keep postponing. Write it down somewhere physical before Sunday ends.

That thing is where the recovered hours are going. Everything that follows is about making that possible. If a full weekend is not available, rotating shifts, family obligations, no clean two-day window, three consecutive evenings work. The point is the pause, not the duration.

Step 3: Move your body

The body has a direct stake in this. The sedentary screen life described in Chapter 19 has a physical cost that is recoverable, and the recovery begins with movement, not as punishment or as a health optimization project, but because a body that moves regularly is a body that sleeps better, concentrates longer, and tolerates the discomfort of the contributing side more readily.

Start with walking. Go outside and move through space without a destination or a soundtrack. Your nervous system needs periodic unoccupied time the same way your mind does, and a walk without earbuds provides both at once. Build from there, any physical practice that you will maintain is the right one.

The time for this comes from the same hours the platforms were using. An hour of movement costs nothing more than the hour you were already spending on the consuming side.

Step 4: Recover your attention

The platforms have shortened your tolerance for anything that does not deliver immediate reward. This is not permanent damage. Attention is a skill, and skills can be rebuilt with practice.

The practice is simple: do one thing at a time, without the phone nearby, for longer than feels comfortable. Read a chapter. Write a page. Work on the project for thirty minutes without checking anything. Cook a meal without background noise. The discomfort at the beginning of these sessions is the attention span rebuilding. It dissipates faster than people expect, usually within a week of consistent practice.

The boredom that arises when the feed is not available is not a problem. It is the raw material of original thought. Let it sit long enough and your brain will produce something. It always does, when given the space.

Step 5: Eat like you mean it

Food and screens have become entangled in the same way that sleep and screens have, each one degrading the other. The mindless eating described in Chapter 19 is not primarily a nutrition problem. It is an attention problem. The food disappears because the attention is elsewhere, and the body keeps sending hunger signals because the brain never registered that eating happened.

The redirect here is simple: eat at a table, without a screen, paying attention to the food. This is not a dietary intervention. It is an attention practice with a side effect of better eating. The meal takes the same amount of time. The awareness of having eaten makes the rest of the evening different.

Step 6: Build something

This is the step that separates a redirect from a detox. A detox removes something. A redirect points the energy somewhere. Step 6 is where the thousand hours go.

Build whatever the redirect from Step 2 pointed toward. Make the thing, learn the skill, handle the admin, set up the system, work on the project. It does not have to be large. It has to be real, something that exists or progresses as a result of your effort, that would not have happened if you had spent the evening on the consuming side instead.

The tools are available. AI handles research, drafting, and admin faster than any previous generation of tools. Spreadsheets are free. Distribution platforms cost nothing. The barrier is not the technology. The barrier is the decision to open something productive rather than something passive when you sit down in the evening. Make that decision once. Then make it again tomorrow.

Step 7: Maintain real relationships

Relationships require time and presence that passive consumption has been quietly claiming. The scrolling hours are often the same hours that phone calls used to occupy, that visits happened in, that letters were written during. Recovering those hours does not automatically rebuild those relationships. You have to point the recovered time at specific people.

Pick one person each week and reach out in a way that requires real exchange, a call, a meal, a walk, a message that asks a genuine question and waits for the answer. The platforms will keep providing the illusion of social connection. Real connection requires the thing the platforms cannot provide: your actual attention, directed at one person, with nothing else happening at the same time.

Step 8: Use technology deliberately

This is the step that did not exist in the original version of this book, because the original version had not yet understood that the tools themselves are not the enemy. Use technology deliberately means: open the device knowing what you are there to do, do that thing, and close it when it is done.

Practically: use AI to handle the tasks that have been piling up. Set up the automation that would get the recurring overhead out of your weekly schedule. Build the financial clarity that has been a background source of anxiety. Use the tools to get things done rather than to fill time. The contributing side of every platform and device you own is available the moment you decide to use it.

The test from Chapter 2 applies here: are you using the tool, or is the tool using you? Is the session ending when you decide it ends, or when the algorithm decides? That distinction, applied consistently, is the entire practice.

Step 9: Find your people

Community provides what individual effort cannot: accountability, shared purpose, and the reminder that other people are working through the same territory. The contributing side of technology is harder to maintain in isolation than in the company of other people who are also trying to build something.

This does not require a formal group or a structured program. It requires a few people who know what you are working on and will notice if you stop. The run club, the maker space, the professional community, the congregation, the handful of friends who ask how the project is going: these are the infrastructure of sustained effort. Build toward them the same way you build toward the other steps: one specific action at a time.

Step 10: Keep the default changed

Everything in this chapter describes a change of default. The default before was passive consumption. The default after is intentional use. The distance between those two defaults is not large. It is exactly the distance between picking up the phone and opening a feed, and picking up the phone and opening something you are building.

The old default will reassert itself. Platforms are designed for exactly that. The practice is not willpower. It is a standing question applied to every session: is this the consuming side or the contributing side? Am I being used right now, or am I using this?

Keep asking the question. The answer changes how you sit down with the device. Over time, the changed default becomes the new normal. The thousand hours stop going to the platform and start going to you.

What the matrix is

The matrix is not a science fiction simulation. It is the accumulation of defaults, the autoplay, the infinite scroll, the notification that arrives whether you want it to or not, the feed that fills any silence you allow. It is the passive side of every tool you own, running continuously, converting your attention into profit for someone else.

Escaping it does not require unplugging. It requires a different relationship to the plug. The same internet that is consuming your evenings is also the infrastructure for everything you want to build. The same AI that will replace your thinking if you let it will amplify your thinking if you use it correctly. The same platforms that are passifying everyone else are the distribution network for anyone who has something worth distributing.

You do not have to choose between the digital world and a life well lived. That is the false choice the consuming side wants you to believe in, because it keeps you passive while you debate it. The actual choice is simpler and available right now: the consuming side or the contributing side. The feed or the project. The algorithm's agenda or yours.

The line is there. You have been reading about it for thirty-nine chapters. Step over it.

Conclusion

What you build in the space that opens up

Remember the couch from Chapter 1? The one with the permanent indentations, the custom-fitted throne built from years of horizontal occupation. The one where I sat in judgment of my stepson for refusing a job because it interfered with Buffy the Vampire Slayer, while being completely unable to argue with his logic because I had done exactly the same thing hundreds of times before. That couch still exists. I sit on it sometimes to read or have a conversation. It no longer has a television to answer to, and neither do I.

Books got written, fifty of them, at last count, plus this one. Fifty books in roughly a decade: that number is not a boast, it is a data point about what a thousand recovered hours a year produces. A business got built. Skills accumulated. Relationships deepened because there was time for them. None of that required genius or exceptional discipline. It only required that the default changed. Not a habit out, a direction in. The screens stayed. What changed was what they were for.

This book has covered a great deal of ground since that couch. The problem has changed enormously since 2014. The default then was television. Now the default has a hundred faces: the social media feed, the smartphone notification loop, the sports betting app, the AI companion, the work messaging platform that follows you to bed, the sleep score that makes you anxious about your sleep. The platforms have multiplied, the targeting has sharpened, the manipulation science has advanced. And the gap between the consuming side and the contributing side of each one has widened, more opportunity on the productive side than ever before, more sophisticated traps on the passive side. It is a harder problem in 2026 than it was in 2014, and a larger opportunity.

But the solution is structurally the same. It has always been structurally the same. Decide what you are going to do with your time before the default fills it for you. Do that thing. Repeat.

What the DO Half of This Book Actually Produced

The second half of this book was not written to balance the first half on a scale. It was written because the title makes a promise that the diagnosis alone cannot keep. Turn Off the TV, Get Off Your Ass, and Do Something is not a self-help book about the dangers of screens. It is a book about what you build when the screens are not running the show.

The DO chapters are specific because vague encouragement is useless. Make something is a chapter because sitting down to produce something, anything, is the core act that the attention economy has been working to prevent. It needs its own chapter, with the Resistance named and the arithmetic laid out, because it is the hinge everything else turns on. Move your body is a chapter because the sedentary screen life has a physical cost that is recoverable, and the recovery is faster than most people expect. Build real friendships, learn a skill that takes years, be somewhere without documenting it, find your community, build something financially real, use technology instead of being used by it, each of these is a specific repudiation of a specific substitution the platforms have been running.

The gaming chapter described how digital achievement substitutes for real accomplishment. Make something is the answer to that. The social media chapter described how parasocial connection substitutes for real relationship. Build real friendships is the answer. The YouTube chapter described how watching expertise substitutes for developing it. Learn a skill that takes years is the answer. The Instagram travel chapter described how curated images substitute for actual experience. Be somewhere without documenting it is the answer. Every diagnosis chapter in the first half of this book has a corresponding DO chapter in the second half. And the diagnosis is no longer purely about absence. Chapter 35 makes the case that using technology deliberately, for your own finances, your own admin, your own decisions, your own work, is itself a form of the redirect. Not giving up the tools. Learning to be the one who uses them rather than the one they use. The substitutions have real alternatives. This is what those alternatives look like.

The Manipulation Is Ongoing

The chapter on manipulation, the supermarkets, the car dealerships, the dark patterns, the advertising that saturates every environment you move through, was included because the digital manipulation does not end when you close the app. The design of commercial environments to override your intentions is a feature of the physical world as well, and the same awareness that helps you resist an algorithmically optimized feed helps you resist an optimized store layout. The skill transfers. The question, whose interests does this choice serve?, is portable.

You will not achieve perfect immunity to manipulation. No one does. The systems running against you have too much data, too much refinement, and too much investment in their effectiveness. What you can achieve is a calibrated skepticism that fires before the impulse completes, a half-second of recognition that buys you the choice. That is enough. That is the whole game.

What My Stepson Did

My stepson did not get that ending. The moment in Chapter 1 was real, the couch, the remote, Buffy the Vampire Slayer, the turned-down job. What happened afterward is that I changed and he did not. More than a decade later he moves from couch to couch, cycles through other people's hospitality, has had stretches involving the legal system, drinks and smokes too much, and reliably explains his situation as the product of everyone around him. The consuming side did not save him. The years of screens and passivity and frictionless substitution produced exactly what the chapters of this book describe: a person who has lost the habit of tolerating difficulty long enough to build anything.

I am not telling you this to be brutal about someone I still care about. I am telling you because the redemption arc version of this story would be a lie, and this book has tried not to tell lies. The mirror moment I described, standing there looking at him on the couch, seeing myself, worked for me. It did not work for him. The difference between us is not talent or luck or circumstance. It is that I stepped off the consuming side and he did not. That is the whole story, and it is not a comfortable one, and it is more honest than the alternative.

The End

The couch is still there. The television is in the closet. The cable box is in there with it. In the time that has passed, I wrote the books, built the business, had the conversations, took the walks, learned the things. The screens were on for most of it. The difference was what they were for.

The tools are the same ones you have. The infrastructure is the same internet you have been scrolling through. The AI is the same AI everyone else is either using or being used by. None of it requires giving anything up. It requires deciding what you are building with it.

The thousand hours are there. They have always been there. They are going somewhere right now.

Decide where. Then start.

Further Reading

This book is the second in a series of four. The Death of Thinking, by Richard Lowe, is the first. It examines the trajectory in which AI dependency systematically erodes the cognitive capacities that make us capable of original thought, independent judgment, and genuine authorship. The Birth of the Augmented Human, the third volume, examines the alternative trajectory, in which the same tools, used deliberately, extend human capability in ways that no previous generation has had access to. Those two books present these as genuine forks in the road rather than inevitable outcomes, and they read most clearly alongside each other and alongside this one.

Stuck in the Middle, the fourth volume, examines what happens to the people between those two trajectories, the ones who did not make a deliberate choice about their relationship with technology and got sorted by the defaults instead. This book describes the choice available at the level of individual habit and platform use. The Death of Thinking and The Birth of the Augmented Human take the question further, into what the choice means for human cognition over time. Stuck in the Middle shows what the middle ground looks like when no choice is made.

The Enshittification of America, also by Richard Lowe, is a companion volume outside the series that steps back further and examines the economic and structural forces that drive platform degradation across every industry, the process by which services built for users are systematically redesigned to extract from them instead. Read together, the five books map the territory from individual digital habits through cognitive consequences through the human cost of indecision through the economic system producing all of it.

The following books go deeper on topics covered in this one. Each is recommended not because the author agrees with every argument in every book, but because each represents serious, substantive thinking about the relationship between technology, attention, and human wellbeing.

Ethan Mollick, *Co-Intelligence: Living and Working with AI* (2024). A professor of management at Wharton who has studied AI tools more systematically than almost anyone else writing for a general audience. Mollick's core argument is that the people who learn to work with AI effectively now will have substantial advantages over those who do not, and that the skill is learnable by ordinary people in ordinary circumstances. The practical framing in this book is the closest existing guide to the contributing-side AI use described in Chapters 2, 16, and 35 of this book.

Cal Newport, *Deep Work: Rules for Focused Success in a Distracted World* (2016) and *Digital Minimalism: Choosing a Focused Life in a Noisy World* (2019). Newport makes the economic and practical case for protecting your attention as a professional asset, and provides a rigorous framework for choosing which technologies to keep and why. Digital Minimalism in particular is the most practical existing guide to reducing digital clutter without rejecting modern technology entirely. Newport's arguments complement Chapters 7, 10, and 37 of this book.

Johann Hari, *Stolen Focus: Why You Can't Pay Attention, and How to Think Deeply Again* (2022). Hari investigates the attention crisis through reporting rather than data analysis, interviewing researchers, technologists, and people whose ability to focus has collapsed. The book is more personally and narratively written than Newport's work, and covers the pharmaceutical, environmental, and dietary dimensions of attention loss alongside the technological ones. The attention crisis described in Chapters 3, 7, and 18 of this book draws on the same body of evidence.

Jonathan Haidt, *The Anxious Generation: How the Great Rewiring of Childhood Is Causing an Epidemic of Mental Illness* (2024). The most influential book of 2024 on the specific harm smartphones and social media have done to adolescents since 2012. Essential reading for anyone with children or who works with young people. Chapter 20 of this book draws on his data and engages with his critics. Haidt's thesis has critics, he engages them directly at anxiousgeneration.com, but the core data on the teen mental health crisis is not seriously disputed.

Tristan Harris and Aza Raskin founded the Center for Humane Technology, whose documentary *The Social Dilemma* (2020, Netflix) remains the clearest explanation of how social media platforms are engineered for compulsive use, told by the engineers who built them. It is not a book, but it belongs on this list. Watching it once is worth more than reading a dozen articles on the subject.

Nir Eyal, *Hooked: How to Build Habit-Forming Products* (2014). This one is on the list for a different reason. Eyal wrote the manual that Silicon Valley used to engineer addictive apps. Reading it tells you exactly how the hook, trigger, variable reward, and investment loop works in the products you use every day. Understanding the mechanism is the first step to resisting it. Chapters 3 and 12 of this book describe the same loops from the user side. Eyal has since written *Indistractable* (2019), which is his attempt to offer the antidote he realized his earlier work had helped create.

Robert Lustig, *The Hacking of the American Mind: The Science Behind the Corporate Takeover of Our Bodies and Brains* (2017). A neuroendocrinologist's account of how the food industry, social media, and consumer culture have exploited the same dopamine pathways to create compulsive consumption. More technical than the other books on this list, but the biochemical grounding is valuable for understanding why willpower alone is rarely sufficient. Chapters 19, 23, and 24 of this book cover the behavioral side of the same mechanisms.

About the Author

Richard is a reformed passive consumer turned active creator who stopped letting screens run his evenings and started using the same technology to build something instead. What friends called "technological suicide" when he unplugged his cable box in 2014 turned out to be the most productive decision of his professional life. That decision launched a decade of using every available tool, AI, digital platforms, automation, to build rather than consume, and turning a thousand recovered hours a year into over fifty books and a successful business.

Richard first documented this redirect in 2016, back when the biggest digital distraction was cable television and the occasional smartphone check. This revised edition addresses the changed landscape of 2026, where we carry the entire internet in our pockets and conduct most of our relationships through screens.

As a professional ghostwriter and author, Richard has helped hundreds of people implement similar digital lifestyle changes. His approach isn't about becoming a technology-hating hermit or rejecting all modern conveniences. It's about remembering that you have a choice in how you spend your time and attention.

When he's not writing books about why you should stop watching other people's lives, Richard can be found living his own life without documenting it for social media. He believes that the most radical act in the modern world is being fully present in your own existence instead of performing it for an audience of strangers.

His motto: "Your life is more interesting than anything on your screen. You just have to decide to use the screen instead of being used by it."

ENEMIES OF YOU

A Series by Richard Lowe

About This Series

<https://enemiesofyou.com>

Something is working against you. Not in the abstract. Not against society or the culture or the country in general. Against you, specifically. Your ability to think. Your ability to pay attention. Your ability to understand what's happening in the world and make good decisions about your own life inside it. Your ability to pass something worth having on to the people who come after you.

This series documents what that something is.

Not one thing. Several things, operating at the same time, from different directions, with different tools. Some of them are commercial. Some of them are political. Some of them are foreign. Some of them were designed specifically to do what they're doing and some of them are just the predictable outcome of systems nobody was watching carefully enough. The result is the same regardless of the cause. Something is eating your capacity to think, to participate, to resist, and to build. This series is about what that something is and what you can do about it.

Each book in the series identifies a specific enemy operating against a specific capacity. The Death of Thinking is about what AI dependency does to your mind when you let it think for you. Turn Off the TV is about what passive consumption does to your time and attention when you let platforms have both. The Birth of the Augmented Human is about the path back to your own capability. Stuck in the Middle is about the geopolitical forces reshaping your world without your knowledge or consent. The Enshittification of America is about the financial engineering that stripped the institutions your daily life depended on and left hollow shells in their place. The Emasculation of America is about the deliberate foreign campaign to demoralize and neutralize the men who would otherwise resist. The Villainization of America is about the psychological operation that turned a nation against its own story.

Seven books. Seven enemies. One argument running through all of them: none of this happened by accident, none of it is inevitable, and all of it can be countered by people who understand what they're actually dealing with.

You can read them in any order. Each one stands on its own. But if you read them together, something becomes visible that isn't visible in any single book: the pattern. The way cognitive erosion feeds civic collapse. The way civic collapse feeds cultural vulnerability. The way cultural vulnerability feeds foreign exploitation. The way foreign exploitation feeds the economic extraction that makes everything else worse. These aren't separate problems. They're the same problem operating at different scales.

The series is written for normal people living normal lives who suspect that something is wrong but can't quite name what it is. Not for academics. Not for policy people. Not for the already-converted on either side of any political argument. For people who are smart enough to understand the world but haven't been given the information in a form that respects their intelligence without requiring a PhD to decode it.

Every book is written at a ninth-grade reading level. On purpose. Not because the ideas are simple. Because clarity is a form of respect. If you can't explain something clearly, you probably don't understand it yourself.

The series is also optimistic. That will surprise you after a few hundred pages of documented disasters, structural failures, and deliberate attacks. But the optimism is earned, not performed. The tools exist to counter every one of the enemies documented in these books. The examples exist. The knowledge exists. The only thing standing between the current situation and a dramatically better one is the decision to act on what you now understand.

That decision is yours.

Enemies of You Series

The Death of Thinking: The Enslavement of Humanity

A diagnosis of what happens to human cognitive capacity when practitioners consistently outsource the parts of their work that require genuine thinking to AI tools. Not in one session or one project, but across months and years of daily practice that removes the demands that were quietly building something. Following composite characters through the specific moments where the pattern becomes visible, this book traces the mechanisms of cognitive erosion: the convenience trap, the illusion of understanding, the death of the wrong answer, and the transfer of epistemic authority that occurs when humans stop standing outside the AI's framing and examining it.

The Birth of the Augmented Human: The Freeing of Humanity

The companion to The Death of Thinking maps the other path. A notebook before the AI is opened. A paragraph written before the structure is requested. A hypothesis formed before the diagnostic tool is consulted. Small choices in sequence that accumulate, over months and years, into a practitioner who is more capable, more original, and more able to surprise themselves than the practitioner who did not make them. The other path is available. This book is the map.

Turn Off The TV, Get Off Your Ass, and Do Something

Most people complain about not having enough time while spending hours every day staring at screens. This is not an anti-technology book and not a minimalism guide. It is an anti-passivity book built around one specific argument: every platform has a consuming side and a contributing side. The device is identical either way. The relationship to it is not. This book is about crossing that line and what waits on the other side.

Stuck in the Middle: Wars, Weapons, and the Forces That Will Shape the Next Thirty Years

Written against the backdrop of a US-Israel strike on Iran that exposed the hollowness of American military industrial capacity, this book connects cognitive decline, civic collapse, private equity extraction, and great power competition into one argument about where the world is heading. Covering missile math, carrier vulnerability, demographic collapse, the Belt and Road as strategic colonization, and the technologies that could solve every crisis on the horizon, this is the book that ties everything else into one coherent warning. And one earned, hard-won optimism.

The Enshittification of America: How Private Equity Destroyed the Things We Love

A documented investigation into how private equity firms systematically acquired beloved American institutions, loaded them with debt, stripped out everything that made them worth visiting, and walked away wealthy while leaving communities with hollow shells of what they once had. Airlines. Restaurants. Department stores. Newspapers. Hospitals. Pharmacies. This book names the firms, documents the playbook, and makes the case that the degradation of American commerce was not inevitable. It was deliberate.

The Emasculation of America: How Russia's Long War Against the American Male Is Destroying the Nation From Within

Beginning with a KGB defector's 1984 warning that nobody heeded, this book traces the deliberate Soviet and Russian strategy to defeat America not through military force but through cultural subversion. Seeding an ideology through universities, amplifying it through social media, delivering it through institutions that now enforce it as policy. Applying academic cult identification criteria to gender ideology, documenting the biological attack through endocrine disruption, and tracing China's acceleration of the same strategy through TikTok, this is not a culture war book. It is a national security argument.

The Villainization of America

America ended slavery, defeated fascism twice, rebuilt its enemies after defeating them, created the largest middle class in human history, and produced more medical and technological breakthroughs than any nation that ever existed. Somehow a significant portion of its own citizens have been convinced it is the primary source of evil in the world. This book documents how that happened, who executed it, and why the psychological campaign to make Americans ashamed of their own country is inseparable from the economic and cultural attacks documented in the two preceding volumes.

Watch the Other Hand: Politics as Cover for the Kleptocracy

While Americans argue about culture war flashpoints and election outcomes, a quieter operation has been moving wealth and power from public hands into private ones at a scale most citizens never see. The political theater is real and exhausting and often deeply felt. It is also doing work for the people whose interests would not survive a population paying attention to what was actually happening. This book documents the kleptocratic capture happening behind the visible politics, names the mechanisms, and traces how the visible politics functions to keep attention pointed elsewhere.

Manufactured Fear: How Crisis Becomes Profit

Every era has its emergencies. The current era has manufactured ones, engineered to maintain a state of generalized anxiety that benefits specific industries and political coalitions. The fear is not invented. The proportions are. This book traces how a healthy capacity for legitimate concern was converted into a permanent state of alarm, names the actors who profit from it, and documents what happens to a population that lives at sustained emergency pitch for years on end.

The Death of Privacy: They Know Everything, You Know Nothing

The surveillance system that the citizens of free societies were promised would never be built has been built. Not by a single state with a single agenda but by a coalition of corporate platforms, advertising infrastructure, data brokers, and government agencies that share the substrate even when they do not coordinate the use. This book documents what is actually known about each individual user, who knows it, what they do with it, and what the absence of meaningful privacy means for political freedom in a society that depends on individuals being able to think and act without continuous monitoring.

The Wrong Fight: How the Climate Response Became the Climate Problem

The climate is changing, the consequences are real, and the response that was supposed to address them has been captured by interests that are using the response as a vehicle for their own purposes. The result is a policy regime that produces consequences which would be unacceptable on their own terms but become acceptable because the alternative is framed as denial. This book separates the science from the policy capture, names the specific failures of the current response, and argues for what an honest climate strategy would look like.

The Quiet War: How America's Adversaries Attack Without Firing a Shot

The hot wars of the twentieth century have been substantially replaced, against the United States in particular, by sustained operations that operate below the threshold of military response. Information operations. Cultural subversion. Economic coercion. Cyber penetration of critical infrastructure. Strategic drug supply campaigns. These are the instruments of the quiet war, and they have been working. This book documents the campaigns currently underway against the United States, names the state actors directing them, and explains why the inability to recognize them as warfare is itself one of the campaigns' objectives.

The Dumbing Down: How American Schools Stopped Teaching Children to Think

American schools have been progressively converted from places where children were taught to think into places where children are processed for credentials. The conversion was not an accident or a failure of execution. It was the predictable outcome of policy choices that prioritized measurable outputs over the difficult work of cognitive development, and that defined educational success in ways that did not require it. This book documents what was lost in the conversion, when the choices were made, and what would have to change to teach thinking again.

The Pattern: How the Enemies of You Work Together

The enemies named across this series are not parallel items on a list. They are a system. Cognitive erosion makes civic collapse possible. Civic collapse creates the conditions for kleptocratic capture. Kleptocratic capture funds the manufactured fear that legitimizes the surveillance state. The surveillance state runs on the educational system that produced citizens who cannot evaluate what is being done to them. Each enemy reinforces the others. None of them can be addressed in isolation. This book is the synthesis: how the system operates as a system, why the standard frame of fix-this-one-problem is itself part of the problem, and what counter-strategy looks like for someone who can finally see the whole shape of the attack.

The Debt Trap: How the Financial System Was Designed to Extract From You

Student loans that cannot be discharged in bankruptcy. Credit cards engineered to keep balances revolving. Mortgages structured so the first ten years of payments are mostly interest. Buy-now-pay-later services that have re-engineered impulse purchasing to operate on an installment basis. Auto loans that now run seven years and underwater within twelve months. Each financial product looks like a service. Each one is a specific design choice about who pays whom over time, and the design has consistently moved in the same direction. This book traces the architecture of consumer debt as a wealth extraction system, names the policies and corporate decisions that built it, and explains why the standard personal-responsibility framing is the cover story that lets the system continue.

The Sick Industry: How American Medicine Profits From Keeping You Sick

The American healthcare system spends more per capita than any other developed nation and produces worse outcomes on most measures that matter. The reason is structural. Chronic illness is more profitable than cure. Symptom management is more profitable than prevention. The food industry produces the conditions that the pharmaceutical industry then medicates. The hospital system bills by procedure, not by health. The medical research apparatus is funded primarily by entities with financial interests in particular conclusions. This book documents the architecture of medical extraction, names the specific incentive structures that produce it, and explains why the conversation about fixing healthcare has been confined to the question of who pays rather than what is being paid for.

The Gambling Machine: How America Made Predatory Gambling the Default

In 2018, sports betting was illegal in nearly every U.S. state. By 2024, it was legal and aggressively advertised in most of them. The expansion was not driven by public demand. It was driven by industry lobbying that succeeded because the public attention was on other issues. The new gambling environment is engineered with the full machinery of behavioral psychology: variable rewards, push notifications, free credits that require deposits, in-game betting that runs faster than judgment can keep up with. The financial outcomes are predictable and documented. The social outcomes are accumulating. This book traces how the legalization happened, who profited, and what is now being done to the people the new system has captured.

The Loneliness Engine: How American Life Was Structured to Isolate You

The third places where Americans used to encounter each other are gone. Bowling leagues, fraternal organizations, churches, neighborhood bars, civic clubs, parent-teacher associations: all measurably smaller, in many cases by orders of magnitude, than they were thirty years ago. The replacements are commercial products that provide the appearance of connection while delivering its opposite. This book documents the destruction of the institutions that made American social life functional, names the economic and policy forces that did the destroying, and traces the consequences for mental health, civic participation, and the basic human capacity to be known by other people.

The Theft of Childhood: How American Kids Stopped Becoming Adults

Children spend more time on screens than in any previous generation, less time outdoors than any previous generation, and reach standard milestones of independence later than any previous generation. The teen mental health collapse that accelerated after 2012 is not mysterious. The mechanism is documented. Phone-based childhood, helicopter parenting, the elimination of unsupervised play, the medicalization of normal developmental difficulty, and the school system's drift toward credentials over capacity have produced a generation that is anxious, fragile, and structurally unprepared for adulthood. This book names what was taken, who took it, and what would have to change for the next generation to get a different result.

Books by Richard Lowe

See books by Richard Lowe at

https://masterofworlds.com

Get free publishing insights and industry updates at

https://thewritingking.substack.com

For ghostwriting and book coaching services see

https://thewritingking.com

Index